A Taste of
HOME

THE PASSAGE
to ending homelessness

THE PASSAGE
to ending homelessness

A Taste of
HOME

120 Delicious Recipes from
Leading Chefs and Celebrities

Foreword by

HRH The Duke of Cambridge

Compiled by Kyle Cathie
Photography by Nassima Rothacker

The Passage Trading Services

This book is dedicated to all clients, volunteers
and staff of The Passage, past and present.

First published in Great Britain in 2020
by The Passage Trading Services Ltd,
St Vincent's Centre, Carlisle Place,
London SW1P 1NL
www.passage.org.uk

ISBN 978 1 52726 516 5

Distributed by Gardners Books Ltd,
1 Whittle Drive, Eastbourne BN23 6QH

Compilation: Kyle Cathie
Design: Ruth Tyson, Ark Design
Food photography: Nassima Rothacker
Food: Becks Wilkinson
Props: Wei Tang
Proofreader: Stephanie Evans
Repro: Altaimage London Ltd.

A Cataloguing in Publication
record for this title is available
from the British Library.

Printed and bound in China by
1010 Printing Pty Ltd.

10 9 8 7 6 5 4 3 2 1

NOTE: photographs at
The Passage of staff, clients,
volunteers and others
were mostly taken before
the outbreak of the
Coronavirus pandemic.

CONTENTS

I am the first one to admit that I am not an excellent chef. The last time I was allowed into the kitchens at The Passage they very sensibly kept me in the role of sous-chef (aka carrot-chopper). On that occasion I 'made' a spaghetti bolognaise (recipe on page 101). The dish smelt amazing – probably because I didn't cook it. But what struck me most was how sharing a hot meal in the canteen at The Passage makes people who are experiencing homelessness feel right at home.

Having a place to call home is precious. All of us will have felt the strain of staying in our homes during the Coronavirus lockdown. But for those without a place to call home, the pandemic has been even more frightening.

Thankfully The Passage made sure there was a route off the streets and into safety. Staff and volunteers have worked tirelessly on the frontline, looking after the most vulnerable in society. At the peak of the crisis, they established a mobile Food Hub, providing hot, nutritious meals every day for over 300 people.

One of the things I will remember from this difficult year is the amazing community spirit and care for the vulnerable shown by our nation. *A Taste of Home* is a celebration of that wonderful spirit. It also marks the 40th anniversary of the founding of The Passage, in a year which has turned out to be one of the most pivotal in their history.

I hope that every time you use this special book you are reminded of that spirit; exemplified in The Passage's ongoing work helping those who are street homeless to find a home for good.

Thank you for buying this book, which marks 40 years of The Passage's work.

We are immensely proud that since 1980 we have helped tens of thousands of people out of homelessness and back into society. However, there is still much to be done to end street homelessness for good.

In 2020 our work was made all the more challenging by the Covid-19 pandemic. All of our lives have been hugely affected by the crisis but, for The Passage and our clients, it completely changed the landscape.

People living on the streets are extremely vulnerable, often with poor physical and mental health and many have complex needs. Even before the outbreak of the crisis, we were experiencing a dramatic 30% increase in demand for our services. Our response had to be rapid and decisive. Working in partnership with other agencies, our frontline teams helped hundreds of rough sleepers into temporary accommodation across London. At the height of lockdown, we set up a Food Hub from our kitchen in Victoria, preparing 350 meals every day, which were delivered 'meals on wheels' style to our clients. We also continued to run our three innovative accommodation projects housing 140 people.

In the months that followed, we assisted many clients to make the transition from temporary to permanent accommodation and to find a place to call home. Through our award-winning Home for Good programme, 97% have sustained their tenancy. We completely transformed our Resource Centre to work safely with around 90 rough sleepers each day, helping them to access benefits, find a job or training and housing solutions – a clear route off the street.

The Passage is blessed with rich diversity; from the amazing courage of our clients to the incredible generosity that so many give in time or financial support, or indeed both. We have wonderful staff who genuinely do care about helping those in society who are most in need.

It is hard for most of us to truly comprehend what it is like to be street homeless. But we all experience times of inner homelessness; bereavement, depression or when we simply feel at a loss. At these times of crisis we turn to those closest to us; family, friends. It is these support networks that catch us; they stop us from falling and ensure that this inner homelessness never becomes physical homelessness. For those without that support, there is The Passage, bringing hope to those who thought all hope had gone.

This special book captures some of that diversity in a year when we celebrated the role of food more than ever and when providing nourishing meals was central to The Passage's response. In addition to recipes from famous faces, we also have contributions from our staff and clients. I truly hope that you find them fun to follow and delicious to eat! I also hope you are moved by the stories about our work.

Of course none of this would have been possible without the contribution of so many people. I would particularly like to thank our Royal Patron, HRH The Duke of Cambridge for the wonderful support he gives to The Passage and for writing the foreword.

Quite simply, street homelessness does not need to exist in 21st century Britain. By buying this book, you are helping those who come to The Passage's door and bringing hope where it is needed most.

Mick Clarke, Chief Executive

FIRST COURSES

John Studzinski, Chair of Ambassador Circle

'As a founding member of The Passage, I have supported and participated
in the charity's work for the past 40 years. Over that time The Passage
has established itself as the caretaker of London's homeless community,
helping over 130,000 people to end their homelessness. I have always
been moved by the organisation's compassion and impressed by its ability
to make a concrete difference to the people who most need its help.
There can be little doubt that, over recent months, The Passage's
response to the Covid-19 crisis will have helped save many lives.
I feel privileged to chair its circle of ambassadors, who all share my
commitment to ending street homelessness, and I hope you enjoy this
special book, published to mark The Passage's 40th anniversary.'

FRAGRANT THAI CHICKEN BROTH

Tom Parker Bowles

Serves 2 as a starter, 1 as a main

500ml good, dark chicken stock

3 pound-coin slices of galangal

2 stalks of lemongrass, first layer of skin removed, then bashed with back of a knife

4 red shallots, peeled (or 1 banana shallot, cut in half)

1 chicken breast

4 tablespoons lime juice

4 tablespoons fish sauce

3-5 bird's eye chillies, chopped

3 red shallots, sliced (or 1 banana shallot, sliced)

This is the sort of soup that feels medicinal, in the very best way. A clear, fragrant broth, scented with lemongrass and galangal, sharp with lime and with a decent chilli kick. It's adapted from a recipe by the great Australian chef David Thompson and is welcome at any time of the day, month or year. It soothes and comforts in the winter, and uplifts and cools in the summer months.

The key to this soup is a good stock, preferably homemade. Also, poach the chicken very gently to ensure it stays soft and tender.

————

Bring the stock to the boil and add the galangal, lemongrass and peeled shallots. Simmer for 10 minutes, turn down the heat then add the chicken and simmer gently for 4–8 minutes, until chicken is done.

Remove the chicken, shred it and put it in a bowl with 1 teaspoon of lime juice, and 1 teaspoon of fish sauce. Set aside.

Strain the stock and bring it back to the boil in the pan for 2 minutes. Add the rest of the fish sauce, lime juice and chillies. Plus the sliced shallots.

If serving as a starter, divide the chicken into two bowls, and pour over the scented broth.

Patrick O'Neill – outreach worker

During lockdown Patrick O'Neill has been assisting his frontline colleagues at Passage House Assessment Centre, which provides Westminster rough sleepers a safe and welcoming place to stay for up to 28 days while a suitable route off the street is found.

Patrick is currently a member of The Community Intervention Team, in partnership with colleagues Scott Hamilton and Josh Brown.

The Community Intervention Team, in partnership with the Victoria Business Improvement District, engages with rough sleepers in The Passage's local area, supporting them to move away from street activity and, in collaboration with local homelessness services, to find a route off the streets.

Prior to joining The Passage, Patrick worked as a carpenter for 26 years in the different areas of construction, building scenery sets for London Theatres and also for John Lewis. Seeking a different role and inspired by The Passage's ethos and Vincentian values Patrick joined The Passage as a volunteer in 2013.

Working with respect and dignity, building trust to assist homeless people realise their own potential is a privileged position which has allowed Patrick to see individuals transform their lives away from rough sleeping.

Serves 4

2 tablespoons
olive oil

1 small onion,
diced (around 225g)

2 carrots, diced
(around 150g)

2 sticks of celery,
finely diced

1 tablespoon peeled
and finely grated
ginger

2 garlic cloves,
finely chopped

½ teaspoon crushed
coriander seeds

½ teaspoon ground
cumin

½ teaspoon ground
turmeric

200g red lentils,
rinsed

1 litre vegetable
stock, homemade if
possible

1 lemon, zested
and juiced

150g chopped kale

½ teaspoon sea salt

¼ teaspoon black
pepper

Good olive oil,
for serving

CURRIED LENTIL
& LEMON SOUP

Robert McCullough

When autumn rolls around and that first sniffle occurs, all you want is soup. Something hearty, healthy and easy to make at the last minute ideally with just a few ingredients, most of which are already in your store cupboard. I started with a languishing bag of red lentils, then added a few flavours I love (especially lemon and kale) to come up with something that in the end was … delicious! The lovely Sophie MacKenzie from the blog Wholehearted Eats tested this with me in our office kitchen, and my staff devoured it with a crusty French loaf and butter. If you don't have kale, spinach is a simple substitute and just as delicious. Now pull on your favourite sweater and make that first soup of the season!

———————

Heat the olive oil in a heavy-bottomed pan over a medium heat. When it's hot, add the onion, carrots and celery. Cook, stirring occasionally, until the onion begins to soften, about 10 minutes.

Add the ginger and the garlic and cook for about 1 minute, stirring often. Once the garlic is cooked, add the spices and cook for 1 minute more.

Tip in the lentils and the vegetable stock, then cover and bring the mixture to the boil. Decrease the heat and simmer for 20 minutes or until the lentils and vegetables are tender.

Add the lemon juice (I started with half the juice and added until it had just the right amount of zing), zest and kale. Continue to simmer until the kale is tender, about 5 minutes.

Season with the salt and pepper, adjusting if needed. Garnish with a drizzle of fine olive oil and serve piping hot.

Serves 4

1 stalk of lemongrass

Chestnut mushrooms

2 peppers, green, orange, yellow or red

1 x 400ml tin coconut milk

Vegetable stock

1 packet laksa noodles

Fish sauce/ponzu/soy sauce

½ lime, juiced

Handful crushed peanuts or chopped coriander

For the spice mix:
2 teaspoon paprika (smoked or unsmoked - up to you)

1 teaspoon ground coriander

1 teaspoon ground fenugreek

1 teaspoon ground turmeric

½ teaspoon ground ginger (or grate in a thumb of peeled fresh ginger if you have some)

½ teaspoon ground cumin

½ teaspoon mustard powder

Pinch of cayenne pepper

1 teaspoon freshly ground black pepper

Pinch or more of dried red chilli flakes (up to you how hot the soup ends up: start gently you can always add more when you taste at the end) or you can deseed and thinly slice 2 fresh red chillies

SPICY ASIAN COMFORT SOUP

Stephen Fry

Well, my Thai soup is really a confection from other people but it's very adaptable; I don't give too precise quantities here, because I go by feel I'm afraid.

———

Bash the lemongrass. Fry it in vegetable oil with some sliced chestnut mushrooms and sliced peppers in a deep frying pan, wok or saucepan – for about 2½–3 minutes.

Mix the spices in roughly the quantities shown and add to the mushroom and pepper.

Pour in a tin of coconut milk and about ⅔ of a mugful of vegetable stock (1 teaspoon of bouillon powder and boiling water) and simmer for 5 or 6 minutes. Drop in a pack of laksa noodles (make sure they're covered by the liquid – they won't take more than 3½ minutes to soften usually).

Now TASTE and according to how you respond, stir in some fish sauce or soy sauce, or – my preference – ponzu sauce, which is Japanese but works incredibly well in this soup, along with a squeeze of lime juice, and seasoning (probably not much needed as there's pepper in the spice mix and soy/ponzu/fish sauces are all nice and salty) – at this stage you can add more chilli flakes/slices of chilli if you don't think it's hot enough: if it's flakes, let them get absorbed for a minute before plating up. You can also add more vegetable stock if the soup seems too thick. If not drink down the remaining stock – it makes a very tasty drink. You can sprinkle over crushed peanuts, or chopped coriander (not me, I loathe fresh coriander, but most people seem to like it), and don't forget to remove the lemongrass.

Enjoy!

CORIANDER, CARROT & ORANGE SOUP

Jekka McVicar

This is a great summer or early autumn soup and, as it freezes well, a lovely way to preserve coriander, which is notoriously difficult.

————

Cut off the coriander roots and wash well, then slice. Roughly chop the green parts.

Heat the oil in a large saucepan over a medium heat. Sauté the carrots and onion for a few minutes until the onion has softened a little. Pour in the stock and add the coriander roots. Bring to the boil and cook until the carrots are tender, about 10–15 minutes. Remove from the heat and allow to cool slightly. Add the orange juice and the roughly chopped coriander leaves.

Purée the soup until smooth, using a stick blender or food processor. Reheat before serving, but do not boil. Taste for seasoning and adjust. Serve with crusty bread.

Serves 2–3

Large bunch of fresh coriander, if possible with the roots

1 tablespoon olive oil

4 large carrots, peeled and roughly chopped

1 onion, roughly chopped

900ml vegetable or chicken stock

Juice of 1 orange

Salt and freshly ground black pepper

In 2019, 3,189 clients visited the The Passage Resource Centre, an increase of over 30% since the previous year.

PUMPKIN & COBNUT SOUP

Nick Sandler

Cobnuts are a type of hazelnut traditionally grown in Kent. They are harvested green from August into September. By October they have darkened to rusty brown and look similar to hazelnuts in the shell. I've seen punnets of cobnuts sold cheaply in local markets, maybe because it takes an intense nut-cracking session to get to the kernel.

By September pumpkins are in full swing and there's a lot of varieties available. Crown Prince has dense flesh with a creamy texture. Try Spaghetti Squash; it looks like a writhing mass of orange noodles when cooked! Come mid-autumn you'll find pumpkins discarded everywhere, adorning shelves, street corners and left to their own devices until, sadly they are stuffed unceremoniously into the compost bin. This recipe tastes great with any of the squashes or pumpkins available in street markets and supermarkets. All you need is an oven, a hob, a stick blender and a large saucepan.

———————

Preheat the oven to 220ºC/Gas 7.

Bake the pumpkin in the oven for around 1½ hours either directly on the oven shelf or in a small baking dish. The pumpkin is ready when it is soft. Cut it in two, scoop out the seeds and discard, then spoon out the soft flesh into a bowl leaving the skin behind.

Gently fry the onion and celery in the olive oil with the lid on the saucepan, stirring occasionally.

After 10 minutes add the cumin, chilli flakes, stock and the pumpkin. Bring to the boil and simmer for a minute or two. Add 25 of the cobnuts to the soup. Crush the remaining cobnuts with the back of a spoon.

Blend the soup until smooth and season with salt and pepper.

If you like your soup creamy add a large dollop of crème fraîche. Sprinkle the crushed nuts on the soup and savour the delicate creamy taste...

Serves 4–6

1 whole pumpkin weighing 2kg or thereabouts, skin cleaned

1 medium onion, roughly chopped

3 sticks of celery, cleaned and roughly chopped

1 tablespoon olive oil

1 teaspoon ground cumin

¼ teaspoon hot chilli flakes

500–700ml vegetable or chicken stock

35 shelled cobnuts, roasted in a low oven, around 120ºC/Gas ½, for 1 hour

100ml full-fat crème fraîche (optional)

Salt and coarse ground black pepper

Serves 4–6

200g leeks, chopped

150g shallots, diced

2 fat garlic cloves, finely chopped

1 fresh red chilli, finely diced

30g ginger, chopped into a small dice

2½ tablespoons coconut oil

160g cannellini beans, cooked and drained weight

350g broccoli, stalky bits diced small, tops cut into small florets

1.3 litres water

3g organic vegetarian bouillon powder

Small handful of mint leaves

Salt

ALLEGRA'S SOUP-ER HEALTHY BROCCOLI, GINGER & CHILLI SOUP

Allegra McEvedy

This soup-er healthy soup is a sure-fire cold-buster! Packed full of vitamin-rich greens and pulses, not to mention those anti-viral, antioxidant, anti-inflammatory super troopers – onion, garlic, ginger and chilli – it's got everything you need to boost your immune system and warm the cockles as the cold weather sets in, or even if you are just in the mood for something hearty and wholesome – whatever the weather!

P.S. Don't forget to use the stalky bits of the brocc in this soup – they are far too good to waste!

———

Sweat the leeks, shallots, garlic, chilli and ginger in the oil, low and slow until soft and sweet.

Stir in the cannellini beans and broccoli stalks and give them a good roll around to coat.

Add the water and organic vegetarian bouillon, then bring to a simmer for 5 minutes.

Blend completely to a purée then put back on the heat and chuck in the florets. Cook for 5-ish minutes until they are just softened, then toss in the mint leaves and par-blitz. Taste and adjust the seasoning and serve.

SIMPLE FISH SOUP

Julia Neuberger

This can be a starter or a main. If you have a lot of fish, it's a meal in itself. Easy to make, it's nourishing because it has so much fish (protein) and tomatoes and herbs give it vitamins. It is a standby for me: whenever I buy fish for a party, I ask the fishmonger for bones or scraps, and that's usually enough for this soup, plus any leftover fish from the party thrown in. And all you need is a big pan (fish carcasses take up a lot of space) and a smaller pan for cooking the soup. If you want to bulk it up even more, do like the French and make croûtons from stale white bread (fry squares with crusts removed in oil till crisp and brown), grate some Gruyère or Emmental cheese to serve with it, and make a rouille (I just use a bit of tomato paste, a crushed garlic clove and a spoonful of mayonnaise. To do it properly, you'll need to make an egg-based sauce and add the garlic and tomato to it).

   All three additions are spooned into the soup when it's ready to serve. For a first course, give small helpings. For mains, you can have bigger helpings and serve it with crusty bread and a green salad.

———————

Fish out all the bones from the cooled stock and save any fish meat from them. Discard the bones and strain the stock into a smaller pan. Add any uncooked fish, heat gently, add in the fish scraps (cooked) after the other fish is cooked, and then the tomatoes and herbs (keeping a little parsley for serving). Season with salt and lots of pepper. Some people add a glass of wine but I don't think it's an improvement. Reheat gently till it's piping hot but not boiling. Taste for seasoning. Serve.

To be even more economical, you can add (at the cooked fish stage) chopped up leftover boiled potatoes and fried onions. Some people start the soup with lots of fried onions but I think that gives it a bitter taste. If it tastes a bit insipid, add a bit more salt, a teaspoon of mustard, and make sure you have some rouille and chopped parsley to add when the soup is served.

Delicious. And, if you get given the fish scraps, amazingly cheap!!!!

Elhadi Adam - Hotel School

Elhadi Adam, known for ease as Adam, was born in Sudan and came to the UK from Italy in 2015 to work in a Middle Eastern restaurant in Durham for six months, before moving to London where he worked at The Palomar and then the Lensbury Hotel in Richmond. He wanted to work as a high-end chef but lost his house and became street homeless. He is now living with friends. One, helping him to create a CV, put him in touch with The Passage. He says Bev from the Client Development Team has been 'very good to me'. He is a graduate of Hotel School.

Serves 8 as a starter or 4 as a main

2 litres fish stock, made from boiling fish carcasses (heads and all) very briefly. Bring to the boil, cook for 30 seconds, then turn it off and leave to cool.

Fish scraps or if none: 600g any white fish, 200g salmon fillet

1 x 400g tin chopped tomatoes

Handful of herbs - parsley, marjoram, thyme, tarragon, dill or any of these separately

Salt and freshly ground black pepper

Serves 4

225g hot-smoked salmon

3 heaped teaspoons
hot horseradish sauce,
homemade preferably

Juice of half a lemon

10g flat leaf parsley,
finely chopped

50ml double cream
(or mayonnaise)

Sea salt and freshly
ground black pepper

HOT-SMOKED SALMON PÂTÉ

Sue Lawley

Living in Westminster I've come to appreciate the work of The Passage at first hand. Homelessness is a national problem but it's felt most acutely in big city centres where those with nowhere to live drift in search of food and shelter. People sleeping rough is a frequent sight in my area. Whenever I see such people, I feel grateful for The Passage. Its volunteers walk the streets at night offering help to those who want it. They take a personal interest in the homeless, helping them re-connect with their families or to prepare them to find work so they can begin to look after themselves. It's the kind of work that requires the special human qualities of patience, selflessness and care, in which The Passage abounds.

My recipe was given to me by Jonathan Norris, the fishmonger in Tachbrook Street Market. Without him Westminster would be the poorer.

————

Flake the salmon off its skin into a mixing bowl. Add the horseradish sauce and mash with a fork. Gradually add the lemon juice, parsley, cream, salt and pepper and keep mashing and tasting. You may need more or less of each of these according to your palate. I like a lot of lemon and my husband likes a lot of salt.

Serve on small squares of hot toast as canapés or more generously as a starter.

markets • Manufacturers
WHOLESALERS corporate film
canteens studios
HOTELS • RESTAURANTS
Caterers Supermarkets
donating generously to
Shelters • HOSTELS DAY
Soup kitchens • CENTRES

THE PASSAGE
to ending homelessness

POTTED FISH

Rebecca Sullivan

I quite often think about homelessness. In fact, in Australia it is women over 50 that are at highest risk in future of being homeless. The women often take time off to have babies. This means they leave their careers, often for so long it's hard to get back into the workforce and then they end up with no supper and, if the marriage breaks down, then they are often left with nothing. It really does scare me, as someone who has always been lucky enough to have three meals a day. A full belly really is so important for nutritional health but also for mental health. I know how I feel when I am 'Hangry'; I am a nightmare, so cannot imagine for a second how it must feel to be in constant hunger.

————

Preheat the oven to 150ºC/Gas 2. Butter four ramekins or small ovenproof dishes.

Heat a frying pan until smoking hot. Coat the fish fillets lightly with olive oil and season with salt. Cook the fillets, skin side down first, for 2 minutes. Flip and cook the other side for another 2 minutes, or until the flesh begins to fall apart. Put into a bowl, remove the skin and discard (or crisp it up in the oven to use as a crisp bread) and then flake the flesh into small pieces. Mix through the fennel and capers, and season to taste.

Divide the fish between the prepared ramekins and press down to level the surface. Cover the fish with two-thirds of the clarified butter. Transfer the ramekins to a shallow ovenproof dish and add boiling water to come halfway up the sides of the ramekins. Bake for 10 minutes. Remove from the oven and leave to cool.

Pour the remaining clarified butter over the fish until it is completely covered. Refrigerate the ramekins for at least 3 hours to set properly.

Serves 4

400g white fish fillets, skin on

Splash of olive oil

2 tablespoons fennel fronds, finely chopped

1 heaped tablespoon salted capers

320g unsalted butter, clarified and cooled

½ cucumber

Splash of raw apple cider vinegar

Crusty bread, to serve

Salt and freshly ground black pepper, to taste

Food Donations

The Passage is supported by any number of donations of food from all over London – City Harvest, Brakes, Fortnum & Mason, Sainsbury's, Prêt à Manger and many more. The Felix Project does a great job in collecting surplus food everywhere in the city, delivering this to charities such as The Passage.

Serves 6-8

1 tablespoon extra
virgin olive oil

250g unsalted butter

2 large onions,
finely sliced

2 garlic cloves,
finely sliced

2 rashers of bacon,
rind removed and
chopped

500g chicken livers
- connective tissue
removed, cleaned
and roughly chopped

Handful of parsley,
chopped

Handful of rosemary,
chopped

Zest and juice of
1 orange

Large slosh of brandy

Large slosh of white
wine

150ml double cream

Salt and freshly
ground black pepper

CHICKEN LIVER PARFAIT

Henrietta Green

The last couple of Christmases, since I have been running British Charcuterie Live and its Awards, I've bought British-made charcuterie as presents. Most people still can't believe we are able to produce such exquisite flavours and textures – I love to prove them wrong!

For years though, I used to make my own, a Chicken Liver Parfait, in huge quantities to give to eager family and friends so my fridge ended up packed with jars and containers of varying sizes for giving away. It's like a pâté, only richer and smoother, and this is a scaled-down version for just a couple of jars but, providing you seal the parfait with butter, it will last about a week and, it follows, the longer you leave it, the more mellow and richer the flavours become.

———————

In a heavy-based frying pan, heat the olive oil with 125g butter and add the onions, garlic and bacon. Cook over a low heat to soften, taking care not to let the onions brown.

Add the chicken livers, parsley, rosemary, orange zest and juice and cook for a few minutes. If the livers look like they might catch, just add another knob of butter.

Pour in the brandy and white wine and continue cooking for a few more minutes, depending on whether you like the livers still pink or well done, this could be anything up to a further 15 minutes. Just check how well done they are by piercing them with a sharp knife.

Remove from the heat and tip the contents of the pan into a liquidiser. Add another knob of butter and the double cream and whizz until smooth (the more of both you add, the richer the pâté but the looser its texture will be).

Season to taste, then pour into a suitable container. Leave to cool, then melt the remaining butter and pour over the top of the parfait to seal. Keep in the fridge for at least a couple of days to mature before serving.

BRAISED CHICKPEAS WITH CARROTS, DATES & FETA

Yotam Ottolenghi

Serve with rice or flatbreads for a vegetarian main course; leave out the feta for a vegan version. Soaking the chickpeas is necessary to achieve the right degree of cooking, so don't be tempted to skip this stage.

———————

Preheat the oven to 180ºC/Gas 4. Drain the soaked chickpeas and set aside.

Put the onion, garlic, ginger and chilli in a food processor, and pulse a few times until very finely chopped but not puréed, scraping down the sides of the bowl as you go. Add the coriander, and pulse a couple more times, just to mix through.

Over a medium-high heat, heat 2 tablespoons of oil in a large, heavy-based cast-iron ovenproof pan with a lid. Add the onion mixture and cook for about 4 minutes, stirring occasionally, then sprinkle in the cumin, cinnamon, dates and tomato paste, and cook for 1 minute more, or until fragrant. Add the drained chickpeas, carrots, bay leaves, bicarbonate of soda, 1.2 litres water and a good grind of black pepper, and bring to the boil, skimming off any froth that comes to the surface. Cover and bake for 2 hours, or until the chickpeas are very soft and the sauce has turned thick and rich. Stir in the lemon juice and 2 teaspoons of salt, then leave to cool for about 10 minutes.

While the chickpeas are cooking, put the feta in a small bowl with the caraway, lemon zest, parsley and remaining 3 tablespoons of olive oil and leave to marinate.

To serve, spoon the feta mixture over the chickpeas and serve directly from the cooking pan.

Serves 6 as a starter, 4 as a main

300g dried chickpeas, soaked overnight in plenty of cold water and 1 teaspoon bicarbonate of soda

1 onion, peeled and roughly chopped

6 garlic cloves, roughly chopped

2cm piece of fresh ginger, peeled and roughly chopped

1 large green chilli, roughly chopped, seeds and all

15g coriander leaves, roughly chopped

75ml olive oil

1½ teaspoons ground cumin

1½ teaspoons ground cinnamon

2 medjool dates, pitted and roughly chopped

1 tablespoon tomato paste

4 carrots (450g), peeled and each cut at an angle into 2 or 3 large chunks

2 bay leaves

¼ teaspoon bicarbonate of soda

Salt and black pepper

1–2 lemons, zest finely grated to get 1½ teaspoons, and juiced to get 2 tablespoons

120g feta, roughly crumbled

1 teaspoon caraway seeds, toasted and roughly crushed

1–2 tablespoons flat leaf parsley, roughly chopped

Serves 4

You will need a china
pie funnel

3 carrots

1 butternut squash

3 tablespoons light
olive or rapeseed oil

½ teaspoon
chilli flakes

1 tablespoon
ras el hanout

1 red onion,
finely chopped

1 fat garlic clove

250g baby spinach
leaves

200g fresh ricotta

120g soft goat's
cheese, crumbled

Salt and freshly ground
black pepper to taste

1 pack all-butter puff
pastry, ready rolled

1 egg

SPARROW PIE
FOR VEGETARIANS

Tom Holland

I wanted to give recipes for a dinner that celebrates British wildlife, and have chosen to theme it around two much-loved, but increasingly endangered, species: the house sparrow and the hedgehog (see page 163).

————

Preheat the oven to 180ºC/Gas 4.

Peel the carrots and squash and chop into small chunks. Place them in a medium sized ovenproof bowl with 2 tablespoons of the oil, chilli flakes, ras el hanout, ½ teaspoon of salt and black pepper to taste. Stir well and when everything is coated put the bowl in the oven for 45 minutes.

Meanwhile put the red onion in a roasting dish and coat it with the remaining oil. Take a fat clove of garlic in its skin and place it alongside the onion. When the squash and carrots have been in the oven for 25 minutes put in the roasting dish with the onion and garlic. Remove everything from the oven after another 20 minutes, by which time the squash/carrots should be tender, and squeeze the garlic clove from its skin, then mash it with a fork and combine with all the other ingredients. Leave to cool slightly.

Blanch the spinach for 1 minute in boiling water and then drain. Leave to cool then chop fairly roughly. Combine the spinach with the ricotta and crumbled goat's cheese. Tip this into a pie dish with all the other ingredients. Make sure everything is combined evenly then put in the pie funnel in the centre.

Cut the pastry to create a lid for the pie dish with some slight overhang. Make a small hole in the centre to fit over the funnel's head. Gently lower onto the pie filling and funnel, trimming any excess.

Whisk the egg in a small bowl and, with a pastry brush, glaze the top of the pie. Bake the pie for 30 minutes then serve immediately with a green salad.

CELERY LEAF & MASHED PARSNIP PATTIES

Jekka McVicar

My aunt, many years ago, introduced me to mashed parsnips which are not only delicious in their own right but also, when combined with celery leaf with its unique flavour, make a lovely starter, light supper or lunch.

———

Preheat the oven to 200°C/Gas 6.

Boil the parsnips in a large pan of slightly salted water until tender. Drain and mash with the onion, garlic and ricotta, and add the finely chopped celery leaf. Beat in the egg yolks and season well with salt, pepper and nutmeg. Whisk the egg whites until stiff then fold into the parsnip mixture. Place spoonfuls of the mixture onto a greased baking dish, sprinkle each one with grated cheese and bake for 30–35 minutes until nicely browned. Serve immediately.

Serves 6

750g large parsnips, peeled and cut into large chunks – discard any very woody cores

1 small onion, finely chopped

1 garlic clove, crushed

125g ricotta or cottage cheese

2 tablespoons finely chopped celery leaf

2 eggs, separated, preferably organic or free range

Salt and freshly ground black pepper

Pinch of nutmeg

Butter for greasing

Grated Cheddar cheese (or any hard cheese)

IF YOU NEED
CLOTHING THIS WEEK,
PLEASE SEE YOUR
KEYWORKER

BUBBLE & SQUEAK

Cherie Blair

I am so grateful for the opportunity to endorse the incredible work of The Passage in their mission to support those who find themselves forced into homelessness. The tireless work of the staff and volunteers who make up this organisation has helped so many individuals who, for various reasons, have found themselves without a roof over their heads. Acting with compassion, respect and treating their clients with the dignity they deserve, The Passage allows homeless people to realise their own potential, helping them to find their feet again.

Having been brought up in Merseyside in the 1960s, homelessness is an issue that I feel strongly about. I was acutely aware of the poverty that surrounded me as a young woman. It was one of the reasons I joined the Labour Party, and I have since engaged with the issue of homelessness through various charities, one of which is the brilliant Emmaus and another, of course, is The Passage.

Whilst I was not born in a shoebox, mine was a modest upbringing, and my mother didn't like us to waste food. I have carried this belief with me through my life, and like to think I have instilled this value in my own children. The recipe I have chosen for this cookbook is Bubble and Squeak, best made with leftovers from a Sunday roast, and an ode to my Liverpudlian roots. The thing I love most is that you can put into it whatever you have, and it turns out slightly different each time! The two basic ingredients are potato and a green vegetable (usually cabbage or Brussels sprouts). After a large roast, it is likely to be a more deluxe dish, with some parsnips, carrots, cauliflower cheese or stuffing added to it; you can also make it from scratch and it is just as delicious.

————

This dish usually begins by frying the onions and some garlic in the olive oil until softened slightly in a large, heavy-based frying pan, then adding the cooked Brussels sprouts and/or shredded cabbage. When the greens are slightly coloured, add the mashed or crushed potatoes. Mash it all together slightly so it is nicely mixed in and push it down so that it covers the bottom of the pan. At this point, the mixture is supposed to make its signature 'squeaking' sound, but I have never had much luck with this. Leave it to catch slightly on the bottom before turning it over to achieve the same effect on the other side.

Serve on its own in wedges, or I like it with a poached egg on top. If you have any leftover meat from your roast dinner this can be served on the side, or some people even like to accompany it with a few rashers of bacon.

The Passage always keeps a ready supply of clean clothes for clients who may not have access to facilities living on the streets.

Serves 8

2 onions, roughly chopped

2 garlic cloves, finely chopped

2 tablespoons olive oil

30 Brussels sprouts, sliced or a whole cabbage, shredded (either use leftovers or pre-cook)

600g mashed potatoes or crushed boiled/ roast potatoes

**Serves 4 as a starter
or light lunch**

500g fresh
tagliatelle

4 courgettes, cut
into long strips

For the pesto:
2 garlic cloves,
peeled

300g basil leaves

150g pine nuts,
preferably
Mediterranean

200g Parmesan cheese,
freshly grated

150ml extra virgin
olive oil

Sea salt and freshly
ground black pepper

TAGLIATELLE WITH PESTO & COURGETTES

Theo Randall

I love making this dish because pesto is very easy to make and brings out the best of fresh basil. It works perfectly with courgettes, and together they make the tagliatelle juicy and flavoursome.

———————

First make the pesto. In a pestle and mortar, crush the garlic with ½ teaspoon sea salt to a smooth paste. Add the basil leaves and pound so the leaves turn to a pulp. Add the pine nuts and crush until smooth. Add 3 tablespoons water and emulsify, then add the Parmesan. Finally, slowly work in the olive oil.

Cook the pasta with the courgettes in a large pan of boiling salted water for about 3 minutes – the pasta should still have a bite.

Meanwhile, warm half of the pesto in a frying pan.

Using tongs, lift the pasta and courgettes from the water and add to the frying pan. Toss with the pesto and add 2–3 tablespoons of the pasta water to loosen the sauce so it coats the pasta strands. Check the seasoning and serve with the remaining pesto on top.

Christopher became homeless in 2010, after losing his job as an accountant. This loss of earnings, coupled with a relationship breakdown, meant he was forced onto the streets where he was sleeping rough for ten months.

   It was not long before Christopher was able to build up a relationship of trust with the team, taking a lead on coordinating the film club at the Resource Centre, and later, becoming a volunteer for The Passage. The commitment shown by Christopher, and the clear positive impact that he had on other clients at The Passage, meant that we were able to support him into a full time role as a paid staff member. This was a huge turning point for Christopher. Being able to use his own experiences to help clients has meant the world to him.

LINGUINE WITH SEAFOOD

Vogue Williams & Spencer Matthews

Vogue's aunty makes this dish and she either makes a brilliant dish or a terrible dish – so it's always hit and miss what you are going to get. So Vogue started making it herself to make up for the misses.

————

Put the shallots and spring onions into a deep frying pan, along with the olive oil, over medium heat and gently fry until soft, then add the garlic and cook for another 1 minute, stirring. Pour in the wine and allow to simmer for a few minutes, then add the stock and continue cooking to reduce the liquid completely.

Add the prawns, along with the sun-dried tomatoes and allow the prawns to cook through if using raw or heat through if you're like Spen! Then stir through the spinach and season to taste.

Meanwhile bring a large pan of generously salted water to the boil and cook the linguine until al dente. Drain, then add to the frying pan with the sauce and mix!

Serves 4

2 shallots,
finely chopped

4 spring onions,
finely chopped

2 tablespoons
olive oil

4 garlic cloves,
finely chopped

175ml dry white wine

500ml homemade
chicken stock

400g prawns
(I would prefer raw but
Spen bought cooked!)

225g sun-dried
tomatoes

250g baby spinach
leaves

Sea salt, freshly
ground black pepper
and chilli flakes

450-500g linguine

The Passage Vincentian values

'We build relationships based on trust.'

Serves 4–6

1 x 400g Gubbeen cheese
(or Camembert)

Carrots

Celery

Apple

MOLTEN CHEESE

Giana Ferguson

This is a perfect dish to meet the children as they come home from school starving – nothing is more nutritious for them than fresh vegetables and cheese… We make our cheese from the milk of our herd here at Gubbeen in West Cork; our land looks out over the Atlantic and the Fastnet Lighthouse, which is the most south-westerly point of the British Isles. We wash our cheeses daily to grow the lovely velvety rind which gives the cheeses their unique flavour.

———

Preheat the oven to 150ºC/Gas 2.

Cut the cheese in half through its equator. Loosely wrap the two halves in baking parchment and place on a tray in a warm (not too hot) oven to melt the cheese until it is molten and runny.

While this is happening, cut into little strips the carrot, celery and some apple. Dunk the veggies into the molten cheese and enjoy!

Per person

100g Taleggio cheese

2 tablespoons
truffle honey

Large bunch of thyme

Salt and freshly
ground black pepper

BAKED TALEGGIO WITH TRUFFLE HONEY

Gregg Wallace

———

Preheat the oven to 200ºC/Gas 6. Place your cheese in individual ovenproof dishes large enough for the cheese to fit in. Spoon the truffle honey on top, add a sprig of thyme to each dish. Season well with salt and pepper and bake for 10 minutes or until gooey. Enjoy with warm crusty bread.

THE PASSAGE
to ending homelessness

GRILLED HALLOUMI SALAD

Hussien Dekmak

Halloumi is traditionally made from sheep's milk but cow's is also used. It is thought to come from Cyprus, where it is often flavoured with dried mint; but it is common throughout the Middle East now – in Lebanon, where I come from, black cumin seeds are often used. It is a good cheese for grilling or frying but it is not a melting cheese, being a fresh brine cheese, shaped and placed in brine.

————

Grill the cheese first on both sides for 3–5 minutes.

Wash the baby spinach leaves, then put them in a bowl and add the sliced tomato as well as the rest of the ingredients. Put the cheese on top and it is ready to serve!

Serves 4

250g halloumi, sliced into 4 pieces

200g baby spinach leaves

1 tomato, sliced

1 teaspoon pomegranate molasses

Half a lemon, juiced

Salt, to taste

Pinch of oregano

Gill King, Fergus Johnston, Lloyd Hastings and John Hague, staff and volunteers at The Passage

Serves 4

225g thin Lebanese cucumbers

1 teaspoon fine salt

1 tablespoon malt vinegar

2 tablespoons extra virgin olive oil

2 tablespoons roughly chopped flat leaf parsley

2 tablespoons roughly chopped dill

175g halloumi cheese, coarsely grated, or feta

4-8 pieces Greek bread, toasted (see introduction)

CUCUMBER & HALLOUMI SALAD ON TOAST

Susie Theodorou

The Cypriots like a dense white bread toast, often sliced from a big round loaf. It's cut about 1–1.5cm thick. Brush with olive oil and toast over charcoal or an open gas flame.

My parents always sought out the thin, short Lebanese- or Turkish-style cucumbers, which are not watery and barely have any seeds, but are packed with flavour. You can substitute the halloumi with feta if you like.

———

Trim the cucumbers and thinly slice into about 0.5cm thick discs. Place in a colander and sprinkle over the salt, toss and leave for 15 minutes. Wash the salt from the cucumbers and pat dry.

Place in a bowl with the vinegar and oil and toss to mix. Add the herbs and halloumi cheese. Toss and taste. If you need salt, add a little more; but only add after tasting as the halloumi or feta may be salty enough.

Pile the cucumber salad on the toast; leave for 5 minutes for the juices to soak into the toast, and serve.

KING·GEORGE'S
FIELD

PASTA ALLA CENERE

Franco Randone

Pasta alla cenere or pasta with ash has minimal ingredients; prepare the sauce while boiling the pasta. The origin of this recipe is unknown. I come from a small town in the middle of the southern mountains in Sicily, where the main economy is agriculture-based and one of the main sources of income is the farming of olive trees, olive oil and pickled black and green olives. The town also faces the volcano Etna, one of the most active on Earth. From time to time during eruptions the ashes are deposited in the town. There has always been a pastoral community; we naturally combine fresh or mature cheese into dishes. As with any Mediterranean recipe *Pasta alla cenere* is made by using simple and locally sourced ingredients. It's created from my background where there's the willingness to combine experience with personal emotion.

Bring approximately 2 litres of salted water to the boil and add the pasta, cooking for around 10 minutes according to the instructions on the packet.

Put the olives in a jar and coarsely blend with a stick blender until you have a homogeneous paste.

Place a large frying pan over a very gentle heat, add the double cream and the blue cheese, stirring until the cheese is completely melted.

Once the pasta is cooked, drain it well and add into the frying pan with the cream and cheese. Add the black olive paste and mix gently before serving.

Serves 4

320g pasta
(approx 80g per person)

60g black olives,
pitted

160ml double cream

160g blue cheese,
cut into small cubes

Salt

Franco Randone - client development - and Marta

Marta came to the UK from Tbilisi to learn English as a doctor. Franco grew up in Buccheri and has a degree in air traffic control, also came to learn English. He did a Masters in Finance at London Metropolitan University and studied at Birkbeck. He spent time working for Toynbee Hall before joining The Passage two years ago. They met in a Foreign Exchange Bureau and are now married with a nine-year-old daughter.

Franco works in the Client Development Department of The Passage, giving clients money advice, helping them to establish bank accounts, navigating complex government benefit schemes such as PIPs. He loves working with people and making life better for them.

Marta speaks Ossetian, Georgian and Russian. Franco speaks Italian; they converse in English. Both enjoy cooking - for Franco it is relaxing and, two years ago, when Marta was making Georgian pizzas, they started videoing them; now they have more than 30,000 followers on their YouTube channel. Marta bakes. Franco loves Khachapuri with Spinach and Cheese.

Serves 4

½ medium watermelon

100g good quality
feta cheese - or more
if you wish

Handful of fresh
mint leaves, roughly
chopped

25g pine nuts,
toasted in a dry pan
until golden

Good quality fruity
olive oil for drizzling

1 lime, halved

Freshly ground
black pepper

WATERMELON, FETA & MINT SALAD

Karen Barnes

This winter more than any other I have been shocked by the increasing number of homeless people on the streets of London, so many of whom clearly have issues with mental health. There's been enough talking about it and it's time for action – change has to happen – and I'm honoured to support the work of The Passage by contributing a recipe to this book.

This is the simplest salad that works well as a starter with some crusty bread on the side, or serve it with a couple of other salads and a plate of charcuterie for the best summer lunch – sublime on a hot day. Feel free to play around with the quantities, adding more feta or mint as you wish.

Next time … swap the pine nuts for toasted chopped hazelnuts. The salad works well with other types of melon, too.

You'll also need … a large platter or plate. Think about the colour: blue, green or white work beautifully with the colours of the salad.

———

Cut the watermelon into 1cm (thinner if you prefer) discs, pick out most of the obvious seeds with the point of a knife – they're not very digestible – then cut the melon into triangles, like wedges of a pie. Leave the skin on as it gives so much colour to the finished dish. Arrange the watermelon decoratively but not too precisely (haphazard is good) on a platter or large plate. At this point I usually cover the plate and put it in the fridge until just before I'm ready to serve the salad as watermelon is one of the few fruits that's better when it's cold.

Five minutes before serving the salad, crumble over the feta cheese, sprinkle with the chopped mint and toasted pine nuts, drizzle the whole plateful generously with olive oil, then squeeze over the lime. Finish with a generous grinding of black pepper (no need for salt as the feta cheese provides a salty-sharp tang), then serve without delay – this isn't a salad that likes to hang around.

NIGVZIANI BADRIJANI

Marta Khabalaeva

Fruits, vegetables and nuts thrive in Georgia, thanks to the good climate. Walnuts are the most popular nut and for this reason there are a lot of very traditional Georgian vegetable dishes that incorporate them. You can find some on our YouTube channel, *Cooking with Franco and Marta*.

Nigvziani badrijani is essential in every festive Georgian banquet. I remember when I was a child and we were invited for some special festive events, eating my favourite *nigvziani badrijani* and black caviar.

Now when people are more focused on healthy eating, I think Georgian aubergine rolls with walnuts is a good choice especially if you grill the aubergines rather than frying them.

———

Wash the aubergines but do not peel them. Cut lengthwise into 0.5cm thick slices and sprinkle the slices generously with salt, leaving to stand for at least 30 minutes, then rinse in a colander, pressing out any bitter juices. Pat dry.

Heat the oil in a frying pan over medium heat and fry the slices on both sides. When they have turned a deep golden brown, remove them from the pan to a plate lined with kitchen paper. Continue until all slices are fried and set them aside to cool. (You can grill aubergines instead of frying for a healthier option.)

To make the walnut sauce, grind the walnuts, garlic and ground coriander in a food processor with some salt and pepper. Gradually add the warm water (around 100ml), stirring to combine. Adjust the consistency of the sauce to taste (use more or less water as you like) and taste for seasoning. Finally add the vinegar and, if using, most of the pomegranate seeds and mix all together.

Spread a generous layer of walnut sauce on one side of each aubergine slice and roll them. Sprinkle with pomegranate seeds before serving.

Serves 4

3 medium-sized aubergines

100ml vegetable oil

For the walnut sauce:
250g walnuts, shelled weight

3 garlic cloves

1–2 teaspoons ground coriander

Salt and pepper to taste

150–200ml warm water (depending on how thick you like the consistency of your sauce)

2 tablespoons white wine vinegar

Seeds from 1 pomegranate (optional)

A lovely example of a client's artwork done while at The Passage.

Serves 4~6 as a meze

250g cooked and
peeled beetroots

75g Greek yogurt

½ teaspoon Aleppo
pepper flakes

30g feta

10g walnuts, bashed
into a rubble

Small handful of dill
fronds, finely chopped

1 teaspoon black
sesame seeds

1 tablespoon
olive oil

Toasted pitta
to serve

Sea salt

BEETROOT BORANI

John Gregory-Smith

Borani is an Iranian style of meze made by combing yogurt with vegetables. In this case, I have used wonderfully nourishing beetroots. They are blended until smooth and mixed with herbs and walnuts. It's very easy to make and is packed with flavour. There is a slight sweetness that comes when using beetroot and it's lovely to offset the flavour with salty feta cheese. They pair beautifully.

————

Tip the beetroots into a food processor and blend until smooth. Transfer to a mixing bowl and add the yogurt, Aleppo pepper flakes and a good pinch of salt. Mix well and scoop into a serving dish.

Crumble the feta over the top and garnish with the walnuts, dill and sesame seeds. Drizzle over the olive oil and serve immediately with pitta.

Serves 4

300g cooked and
peeled beetroots

2 garlic cloves,
crushed

Lemon juice
(measure by taste)

½ teaspoon
cumin seeds

50g tahini

Salt to taste

BEETROOT HUMMUS

Hussien Dekmak

Hummus is the Arabic word for 'chickpeas' and it is eaten all over the Middle East, and now the rest of the world too. The earliest recipe comes from Egypt in the 13th century. Here, I've substituted the chickpeas with beetroots for a change.

————

Put the beetroot and garlic in a blender and add the salt, lemon juice, cumin and tahini. Blend them together into a smooth mixture (add some water to soften the mixture if it's too thick).

Serves 8-10

150g white onion, chopped

Fresh lime juice, to taste

800g avocados, stoned

100g fresh coriander, chopped

90g serrano chilli deseeded and chopped, or to taste

Pomegranate seeds, to taste

Requesón (white moist cheese - the Mexican version of ricotta)

Corn tortillas, cut in triangles and fried, or *maíz tostadas*

Salt and freshly ground black pepper, to taste

NATIONALISTIC GUACAMOLE

Martha Ortiz

———

Soak the onion in the lime juice for half an hour and then drain. Carefully mash the avocado in a bowl or molcajete (a Mexican traditional lava-stone mortar with pestle). Add the coriander, onion and chilli. Season with salt and pepper.

Serve the guacamole in an dish garnished with the pomegranate seeds, the requesón cheese, and the tortilla triangles.

Per person

5 green asparagus spears

Olive oil or butter

Cream (optional)

Sea salt and freshly ground black pepper

ASPARAGUS NE PLUS ULTRA

Bob Flowerdew

With decades of growing a huge supply of FRESH asparagus I'm satisfied this highly nutritious spring green needs the briefest cooking and little accompaniment save possibly a coating of fine butter. All else is superfluous, unless the asparagus is not truly fresh, in which case sauces and even admixtures of ham, chicken or cheese may help.

———

Wash and dry your asparagus spears.

Cut off the very tips, say the top 2cm and put these aside. Next cut another 2–3cm long length off each spear and put these aside separately.

Boil the remaining stumps (10cm) of the spears in minimal water for 15 minutes, drain then rub through a sieve to remove the tough fibrous bases, leaving a purée.

While the stumps are boiling, gently fry the 2–3cm lengths in olive oil, or even more gently in butter, and keep warm until the purée is ready.

Once ready put the purée back over the heat, adding pepper and salt, blending in butter, cream or olive oil to taste . Just before serving mix in the fried lengths and garnish with the raw tips coated with rock salt and coarsely ground black pepper.

ASPARAGUS RISOTTO

Nour Dakoba

I love Italy and have loved eating even more when I've had risotto made there. It's important to stir the rice while it is cooking to get a creamy risotto; and you can add peas too if you like. Try and find the best quality Parmesan you can.

―――――

Bring a pan of water to the boil and drop in the asparagus for 4–5 minutes; when tender, drain the spears and chop into pieces 2cm long.

In the same pan, bring the chicken stock to the boil and keep it on a low simmer.

Melt two-thirds of the butter in a large saucepan over a medium heat and cook the shallots until they are soft but not coloured. Then tip in the rice, along with a good pinch of salt and stir for about 3 minutes until the rice turns translucent. Increase the heat and add the wine. When it has evaporated, add in a couple of ladles of hot stock and reduce the heat; keep stirring until the liquid is absorbed. Continue adding ladlefuls of stock and stirring until the rice is almost cooked. Mix in the asparagus, remaining butter and Parmesan and season with salt and pepper.

Serve in bowls and sprinkle with Parmesan.

Serves 4

12 green asparagus spears, trimmed

2 litres homemade chicken stock

75g butter

200g banana shallots, finely chopped

400g risotto rice (arborio or carnaroli)

200ml dry white wine

60–75g Parmesan cheese, grated, plus extra for serving

Salt and freshly ground black pepper

The Passage Vincentian values

'We assist homeless people to realise their own potential to transform their lives.'

CRACKLING RICE PAPER ASPARAGUS ROLLS

Ken Hom

Asparagus, native to the Mediterranean, has been cultivated in the West since antiquity. Now widely grown throughout the world, it is a popular vegetable, prized for its delicate flavour. In this recipe, I use rice paper that is made from rice flour, water and salt. I love its ability to envelope food with a crispy crackling skin while keeping the food moist. It is a simple dish to make, a vegetarian treat.

———

Trim the asparagus to 14cm and discard the tough ends. Blanch the asparagus in a large pan of boiling, salted water for 3 minutes. Drain immediately and plunge into cold water to stop it from cooking. Drain well.

Combine the asparagus with the salt, pepper, olive oil, chives, spring onions, fresh coriander and sun-dried tomatoes.

Make the flour paste by mixing the flour and water together.

When you are ready to make the rolls, fill a large bowl with warm water. Dip a rice paper round in the water and let it soften for 1 minute. Remove and drain on a linen teatowel.

Place 3 asparagus spears and a little of the tomato-herb mixture on the rice paper and immediately roll the edge over the asparagus, fold in both sides of the rice paper, and continue to roll to the end. Seal the end with a little of the flour paste mixture. The roll should be compact and tight, rather like a short, thick finger cigar about 7.5cm long. Set it on a clean plate and continue the process until you have used up all asparagus. (The rolls can be made ahead to this point; cover loosely with a dry linen teatowel and refrigerate for up to 4 hours.)

Heat a wok or large frying pan over a high heat until it is hot. Add the oil, and when it is smoking, turn the heat down to medium and pan-fry the rolls a few at a time, until they are golden brown. They have a tendency to stick to each other at the beginning of the frying; do not attempt to break them apart should they stick together. You can do this after they have been removed from the oil. Continue frying until you have cooked them all. Drain on kitchen paper and serve at once.

Serves 4

450g asparagus spears

1 teaspoon salt

½ teaspoon freshly ground black pepper, to taste

1½ tablespoons extra virgin olive oil

3 tablespoons finely chopped chives

2 tablespoons finely chopped spring onions

1 tablespoon finely chopped coriander

3 tablespoons finely chopped sun-dried tomatoes

For the flour paste:
3 tablespoons plain flour

3 tablespoons water

1 packet of Bánh Tráng dried rice paper (22cm rounds)

150ml olive oil

Serves 4

450g ceps

1 small onion,
chopped

1 garlic clove,
chopped

50g butter

1 large tomato,
deseeded and
chopped

3 teaspoons
mild paprika

4 tablespoons
soured cream

Lemon juice

Salt

PAPRIKA MUSHROOMS

Roger Phillips

My favourite spice is paprika so I naturally gravitate towards it as my first choice for flavouring a mushroom dish. Whilst I was working on my *Wild Food* book, I made copious use of Jane Grigson's mushroom cookery book, and inspiration for this dish comes from her. Before publishing my version, I asked Jane if she was happy for me to follow her recipe idea, and her response was as follows: 'I based my recipe on traditional Viennese writings, so I am totally happy for you to base one of yours on me.'

The best mushrooms for this dish are ceps but if they are not readily available it is fine to substitute ordinary shop mushrooms, or the newly more available King Oyster mushrooms, but be sure to select fairly large, firm specimens.

————

Chop the mushrooms into bite-sized pieces. Cook the onion and garlic in the butter until soft and golden. Stir in the tomato and bubble everything together for a few moments before adding the paprika, followed by the mushrooms. Cover and cook for 4 minutes, add salt to taste, then stir in the soured cream. Allow it all to simmer gently for a few minutes to thicken the sauce, then season with lemon juice and serve immediately.

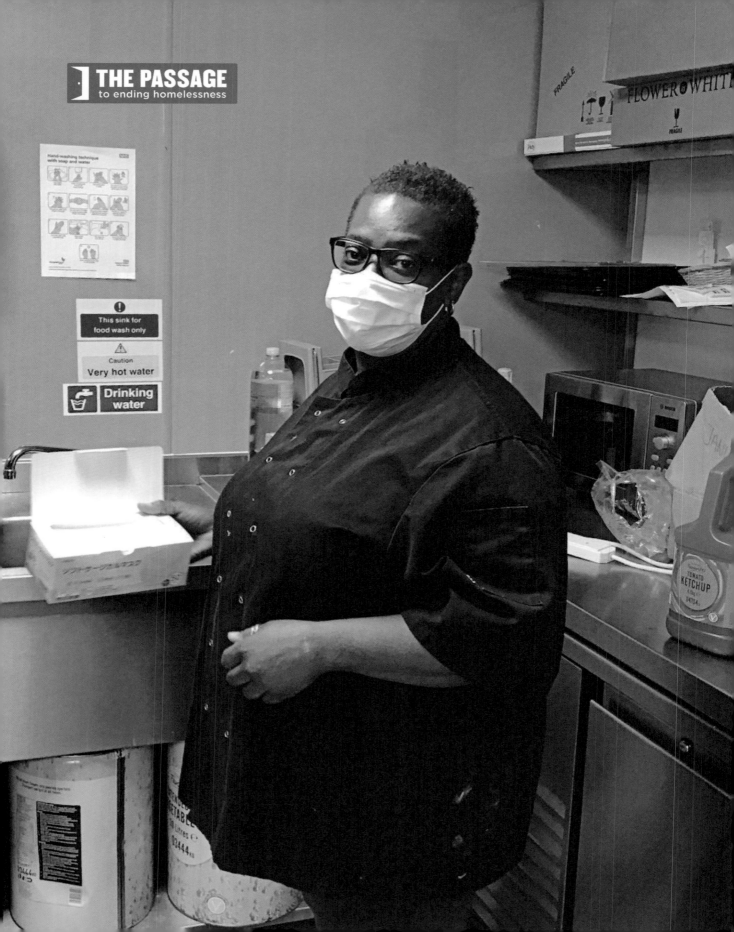

BAKED BEANS

David Dimbleby

———

When I am eating alone I have one favourite recipe. Open a large tin of Heinz baked beans. Stir with a spoon to mix the beans and the tomato sauce. Add a generous dose of Worcestershire Sauce and mix in thoroughly. Eat from the can. (As an occasional luxury, add a raw egg.) Delicious.

Claudette Dawkins - The Passage Head Chef

'No two days working at The Passage are ever the same' says Claudette, the calm, friendly and super-organised Head Chef. She is allowed to be creative over the food that she and her chef Nour provide. Hence she had worked here for over 21 years.

Claudette was born in the UK of Jamaican parents. After school she worked in a canteen in Liverpool Street, grabbing every chance for training, before moving to a restaurant in Camberwell. The opportunity came up for her to work at Langan's Brasserie in Mayfair, first as chef de partie on the veg section, moving onto the grill and finally on the pastry section. Whilst there, she also completed her NVQ Level 3.

From Langan's Brasserie, a job as a Head Chef at The Passage came up and Claudette was encouraged to go for it. In May 1999 she went for the interview and was offered the job both on the same day. Since being at The Passage she completed her diploma in Food Hygiene Management and now has the official title of Claudette Dawkins MRSPH.

The food offered at The Passage range from good hearty home cooked food, to lighter options like salads. The kitchen also caters for vegans and people with dietary requirements. The menu at The Passage tries to reflect seasons and celebrations like fish Fridays and St Patrick's Day. One of Claudette's favourite foods is Jerk Chicken that she cooks on a traditional Jerk Pan.

Her goal is to leave work each day feeling she had given the clients really good food. She needs to reflect that she and Nour did their best for the clients.

The Passage benefits from donations from many food retailers and suppliers. Claudette has a duty of care to ensure donations - and any food we cook and serve - are safe to eat.

Claudette observes that The Passage is a fortunate charity that is able to give clients decent portions of food, which will sustain them.

Her budget annually is £67,000. Claudette and Nour used to cook a full English breakfast and a hot lunch daily, until Coronavirus. Now they are making food parcels for over 300 homeless people in London seven days a week. The food parcels consist of breakfast items, a sandwich for lunch, soup and a hot meal and snacks.

In her time at The Passage Claudette has seen a big rise in the number of clients coming in, while their concerns are worked through. She has vast respect for each and every one of them.

When she returned to work in 2000 from maternity leave, she was incredibly touched by comments from the clients and even a gift of a blanket that was given to her for her new-born. 'We're all the same', she says; 'When we cut we bleed'.

Serves 4

4 large oranges

4 small spring
onions

Chilli flakes

4 tablespoons
olive oil

Pinch of salt

SICILIAN ORANGE SALAD

Franco Randone

Orange salad is popular in winter in Sicily, where it is commonly made with local orange varieties. There are many versions of this Mediterranean dish and this is my mother's recipe. It is very simple and quick, ideal for people who love salad and want to use seasonal produce. This salad can be served as an appetiser, as part of a meze, to refresh the palate between courses, or on its own when having a light dinner.

———

First peel the oranges and cut the segments into small pieces. Finely slice the spring onions and mix them with the oranges in a bowl. Add chilli flakes to taste, along with a small pinch of salt. Then stir in the olive oil and mix.

Serves 2-3

1 rasher of bacon

1 egg yolk

90g crème fraîche

Parmesan cheese, grated

Salt and freshly ground black pepper

Poached egg (to serve, 1 per person)

Carrot tops (the fronds), chopped - parsley or tarragon could be used

EGG CARBONARA

Lewis Macleod of Rude Health Café

We all have our favourite brunch treats, whether it's eggs Benedict, eggs Florentine, French toast and bacon or the full English. This is a slightly different poached egg dish with the classic flavours of carbonara without the carbs of pasta.

———

Preheat the oven to 170ºC/Gas 3.

Drop the bacon into a frying pan over a medium heat with a little oil. Once the rasher is cooked through, to get it crispy, put it in the oven until brittle and brown. Remove and dice.

Bring a small pan of water to the boil and select a heatproof bowl that will sit on top. Put the egg yolk and the crème fraîche into the bowl and beat together.

Put the bowl over the hot water, and once boiling turn down the heat to medium – if it is too hot you'll scramble your egg. Also, make sure that the water does not touch the bottom of the bowl. Now you need to stir the mixture constantly until it thickens and the egg is cooked. This will take a little time so have patience (about 15 minutes). The hotter your pan of water the faster the egg will cook but you run the risk of scrambled egg.

Once happy with the thickened sauce, add the grated cheese. For this volume you'll need about a handful. Melt the cheese into the sauce, add the bacon and some black pepper. Then season to taste with salt.

If the sauce is too thick at this point, you can add a little warm water to loosen it.

Serve the sauce over poached eggs and top with carrot fronds.

TURMERIC & PRESERVED LEMON HUMMUS

Rachel Higgins of Rude Health Café

Hummus is an internationally loved dip, which has perhaps become rather fashionable over recent years. High in protein from the chickpeas and healthy fats from sesame and olive oil, what is there to stop us from adding even more health benefits to this delicious dip? Turmeric has been used in South East Asian cuisine for centuries but, in true British style, we like to suddenly brand it as the new 'superfood' due to its anti-inflammatory properties and ability to improve brain function. As a result we try and shove it in everything possible … so why not add it to hummus?! Life-changing properties aside, either fresh or ground, it brings a subtly earthy and aromatic flavour with notes of orange and ginger, not forgetting the vibrant yellow colour it brings which instantly draws us to it. When paired with preserved lemon, the citrus notes of the turmeric are enhanced and bring a new-found freshness to hummus which is usually considered as a rather rich-tasting dip.

———

Pop everything into a powerful blender, whizz until smooth while slowly adding water until the desired consistency is reached. Check the seasoning and add more salt if required.

Serves 4

1 x 400g tin chickpeas, rinsed

3 roasted garlic cloves (drizzle the unpeeled cloves with a little olive oil, loosely wrap in foil and roast in the oven at 200°C/Gas 6 until soft, then pop the cloves from the papery skin)

3 tablespoons tahini

2 preserved lemons

½ tablespoon ground turmeric OR 1½ tablespoons grated fresh turmeric

Good pinch of salt

2 tablespoons olive oil

Water to thin

Serves 3

500g full-fat
Greek yogurt

1 teaspoon salt

40g hazelnuts

6 ripe figs

Drizzle of extra
virgin olive oil

Big pinch of sumac

LABNEH, TORN FIGS, TOASTED HAZELNUTS, SUMAC, OLIVE OIL

Fergus Snell of Rude Health Café

Due to the simplicity, each ingredient has a huge role. This isn't about technique, it's all about quality produce and of course the late summer season – which makes it even more special. The combination of ripe jammy figs with salty labneh is as perfect as it sounds. Toasted hazelnuts give depth and a welcomed texture whilst citrusy sumac transports you to the Middle East and cuts through the creaminess of the labneh. Finally, a generous glug of peppery extra virgin olive oil binds the whole dish, adding a beautiful vibrant green. The only element that needs time is hanging the labneh, otherwise this combination of beautiful ingredients can be put together in minutes. If the figs are at their peak, they can be torn into thirds rather than slicing, this reflects the simple and rustic nature of the dish.

————

Mix the salt with the yogurt. Suspend the mixture in a cheesecloth over a bowl overnight in the fridge.

Roast the hazelnuts until nicely toasted. Rub with a clean kitchen towel to remove the husks. Crush the hazelnuts to break them coarsely but not into a powder.

Tear the ripe figs into thirds.

Just before serving, spoon the labneh onto three plates. Top with the torn figs, the roasted hazelnuts, a drizzle of good extra virgin olive oil and a big pinch of sumac.

Serves 4

6 heritage tomatoes, ideally 2 red, 2 green and 2 yellow

2 slices soda/brown bread

1 garlic clove

2 avocados

Tabasco, to taste

Bunch of crisp radishes

About 200g feta cheese

Sea salt

For the dressing:
Olive oil

Squeeze of lemon juice

1 garlic clove, crushed

Salt and pepper

A SIMPLE, COLOURFUL VEGGIE SALAD

Petroc Trelawny

My life got better – and healthier – when a fantastic independent greengrocer opened near me a few years back. The variety of fruit and vegetables on display looks and smells gorgeous and is somehow life-enhancing. Best of all, there is no packaging, everything is loose, so you can choose and buy what you want, a single tomato, a handful of herbs, eight new potatoes.

Since then, this simple salad has become a regular starter when friends come around. It takes minutes to prepare, and the rich colours of its ingredients almost dazzle, the varied tastes and textures contrasting brilliantly.

———

Chop the tomatoes finely and dress them.

Toast the bread, halve each slice, cut off the crusts and rub garlic into one side. Then mash the avocado and stir in a few drops of Tabasco. Using a mandolin, slice the radishes as thin as possible, so they appear almost translucent.

Use big, white plates to serve, in your mind dividing them into three sections. Place the tomatoes in one section. Lay the sliced radishes out in another and sprinkle them with the salt. Place the toasts in the remaining area, and spoon the avocado mix over, sprinkling liberally with crumbled feta. Congratulate yourself for serving a dish that is both healthy and beautiful.

Serves 1

Handful of baby spinach and/or romaine

1 avocado, sliced

4 cherry tomatoes

Small handful of crumbled feta

Half a handful of pine nuts

For the dressing:
125ml virgin olive oil

60ml balsamic vinegar

Juice of half a lemon

SIMPLE SALAD

Paul McCartney

———

This is a simple salad that I often enjoy. I start with lettuce which is usually baby spinach or romaine. Then I slice little cherry tomatoes and slice the avocado pear and add them to the lettuce. I then crumble in some feta cheese and sprinkle over and top this creation off with pine nuts.

For the dressing I also like to keep it simple so it is just some light virgin olive oil mixed with balsamic vinegar and lemon juice. Pour over, mix, serve and enjoy.

FANTAIL ROLLS

Shaun Hill

My own bread-making pedigree stems from the opening of my first restaurant in 1982, a well-regarded but financially dubious place in Stratford-upon-Avon. I'd never made bread and there was at the time no decent local bakery so *The Sunday Times Book of Real Bread* was purchased and every recipe tried out in turn. The most successful was a fantail roll from New England and I bake and serve it still. The roll is very light and breaks into segments crisp on the outside but soft otherwise, ideal for mopping sauces.

These were originally called buttermilk rolls and the recipe called for buttermilk. I find that the cultured buttermilk for sale is closer to yogurt than the original ingredient which is a by product of butter making and a thin, sharp liquid, ideal for this recipe. I have for years substituted skimmed milk with a pinch of cream of tartar and recommend you do the same.

————

Preheat the oven to 220ºC/Gas 7.

In a bowl dissolve the yeast and honey in a little of the skimmed milk and leave for 10 minutes somewhere warm to froth. Pour this plus the remaining milk onto the flour and salt and mix to a dough. Knead for 5 minutes – less if you are using a mechanical mixer. Cover with cling film and leave somewhere warm and draught-free to prove, about 1 hour but it varies; the dough should be puffed and light. Melt the butter.

Knock back the dough. Knocking back sadly isn't a jolly drinking expression but involves kneading the dough to deflate it so that the proving process can restart. Divide the dough into two pieces and roll out to 3mm. Brush the top surface with melted butter. Cut the dough into strips 5cm wide and lay these strips on top of each other in piles four strips high. Cut them into squares of 5cm.

Pinch 1 corner of each square together to seal the squares then stand the squares, pinched side downwards, in buttered Yorkshire pudding tins. Leave to rise for 1 hour then brush with the beaten egg.

Bake in the oven for 15 minutes by which time they should be golden brown.

Makes 15-20 rolls

25g fresh yeast

1 teaspoon honey

450ml skimmed milk, with a pinch of cream of tartar added

750g strong white flour - good quality, remember bread is 99% flour - I use Shipton Mill or Doves Farm

1 teaspoon salt

75g unsalted butter

1 medium egg, beaten

ADJARIAN KHACHAPURI

Marta Khabalaeva

Serves 4

For the dough:
500g strong white flour

1 teaspoon salt

300~350ml warm water

1 teaspoon sugar

7g dried yeast

1 egg

30~50ml vegetable oil

For the filling:
650g mixed cheese (mozzarella, cottage cheese, grated Cheddar etc. You can use your own favourite cheese)

80ml milk

2 eggs

To finish:
4 egg yolks

4 tablespoons softened butter

I was born in Tbilisi, capital of Georgia (then still in the USSR). Georgia was special; it was known as 'paradise', a dream holiday destination for all Soviet people because there is a very nice climate, seaside (Black Sea) and — most importantly – delicious Georgian cuisine: *khachapuri, chikhirtma, chaxoxbili, khinkali, churchkhela, gozinaki, mzvadi, pxali, nigvziani badrijani, sazivi, lobio, mzadi.* All these dishes were very famous in all USSR.

This recipe is a gorgeous boat-shaped 'pizza' with cheese, egg and butter in its centre, from Adjara, a region on the coast of the Black Sea, perhaps the reason they are boat-shaped (all other Georgian *khachapuri* are round, like pizza). I believe one day Georgian *khachapuri* will become as popular as Italian pizza. Try these and you'll understand why.

I was lucky to have mother who was one of the best pastry chefs in Tbilisi, was excellent at cooking any food and had very good taste. I ate only the most amazing food every day.

Not surprisingly I married a man who is very good at cooking, Franco is Italian (Sicilian), and often I am sorry for other people who can't try his cooking! To let people enjoy tasty Georgian and Italian food we created a cooking channel on YouTube: *Cooking with Franco and Marta.* We are trying to make our recipes as simple and clear as possible.

————

Put the flour in a large bowl, add the salt and mix together.

In a small bowl put half of the warm water, the sugar and dried yeast and mix together. Leave to rest for about 10–15 minutes or until it is bubbling and foamy.

Drop the yeast mixture into the large bowl, add the egg and mix together. Add the remaining water little by little until you have a soft dough (you might need less water). Then add the vegetable oil (a few tablespoons) to make the dough softer.

Cover the bowl with cling film and leave in warm place to rise for at least 1 hour or until it is doubled in size. Divide the dough into 4 equal pieces each around 200–250g. Mix the grated cheese with the milk and 2 eggs in a bowl and divide the filling into 4 equal parts.

Preheat the oven to 240ºC/Gas 9 (or your hottest oven setting).

Roll out each ball dough into an oval (or simply shape using your hands). Fold in the two long sides of the oval to form a boat shape, then twist the ends into a point to seal and prevent the sides from unfolding. Place on a baking sheet.

Fill the centre of each boat with the cheese mixture. Bake until the crust is golden and the cheese is bubbling, about 10–15 minutes. Take the baking sheet out of the oven, crack 1 egg yolk into the middle of the boats and return to the oven for 2–3 minutes more. The yolk should still be runny. After removing from the oven, put 1 tablespoon of soft butter on top of the filling. Mix the egg into the hot cheese and butter. Eat while still hot.

SUMMER ROLLS

Sadie Frost

I love this recipe as it has so many tangy flavours - it's also really healthy and incredibly moreish.

I have always supported charities that help the homeless. It's ridiculous that, in this day and age, anyone should not have a roof over their head! I work very hard with homeless people in my area, trying to give them support and a voice so they can be heard.

———

Chop up all the salad/vegetables and put them in a bowl, then mix them together. Heat some water in a large frying pan then turn off the heat. Place the summer roll wrappers into the water for 10–15 seconds until they are soft. Remove from the water and put them, separated, on a plate. Place some of the mixed filling ingredients in the centre of each wrapper and roll them up to make four summer rolls.

For the dipping sauce, put all the ingredients into a bowl and mix. Season to taste. Serve in a small bowl for everyone to help themselves, along with the wrappers.

Makes 4 rolls

2 carrots,
cut into ribbons
with a julienne
peeler

1 red pepper,
cut into thin strips

1 cucumber (small),
cut into ribbons

4 spring onions,
cut into ribbons

Small bunch of
coriander leaves,
stripped from
the stalks

Small bunch of mint,
leaves stripped from
the stalks

Tofu, marinated in soy
sauce and ginger

Handful of alfalfa
sprouts

4 summer roll wrappers

For the dipping sauce:
100g smooth peanut
butter

1 tablespoon
soy sauce

½ teaspoon
chilli flakes

Shawn Harris - client

Shawn got into drugs and alcohol and couldn't escape them. As a result he lost his job and had family issues, which led to him becoming depressed. He spent his life amongst the wrong crowd and is easily led, he says. He walked away from home and started sleeping rough in Manchester, Cardiff, Leeds and other northern towns before coming to London. He'd heard about The Passage and, arriving at King's Cross, he walked down to the Centre in 2017.

With support from The Passage, he's been off drugs completely for 2 years, off alcohol for 6-7 months. He recently moved into private rented accommodation. His next goal is to get a job.

MAIN COURSES

Sadiq Khan, Mayor of London

'Helping rough sleepers in London access vital services and get off the streets has been a top priority for me as Mayor, which is why I'm pleased to support this brilliant new recipe book. Charities such as The Passage play a crucial role in helping some of the most vulnerable people in our city and I'm proud to stand side by side with them in the mission to end homelessness. I encourage Londoners to buy this book, brush up on their culinary skills and get cooking for a good cause!'

CHICKEN & POMEGRANATE PLOV

Caroline Eden

It is said that the Chinese eat with their stomachs, and the Japanese with their eyes, but I would argue that Uzbeks do both. Their national dish is *plov*, a delicious and satisfying meal that looks remarkable too. Cooked outdoors, over hot coals in a giant cauldron, it is a layered rice dish consisting mainly of onions, carrots and meat, which is then served dotted with ingredients such as red barberries, raisins and quails' eggs. Spiced very sparingly with cumin, paprika, cayenne and perhaps turmeric, *plov* relies on the qualities of its main ingredients. It is a sociable dish, too, eaten communally from a large plate or lagan placed on the table, with everyone helping themselves.

But *plov* is eaten all over the former Soviet Union, taking different forms. This *plov* is inspired by a dish I ate in Azerbaijan. Light, easy to make, healthy and highly nutritious the pomegranate seeds are rich in antioxidants, potassium and vitamin C and the chicken full of protein. It works really well for a family weeknight dinner.

————

You'll need a heavy-bottomed pan, such as a large cast-iron casserole, with a close-fitting lid (or some foil to fashion one).

Start by putting the rice into a bowl of cold water to soak. Next, warm the oil over a medium-high heat, then once hot add the carrots, onions, cumin seeds and ½ teaspoon of black pepper and cook until softened.

Next, layer the chicken on top of the vegetables, let the steam cook the chicken, but do not stir as you want the layers to remain. To cook through, gently turn the chicken pieces over once or twice, then once white and cooked, sprinkle over the cayenne pepper and season with salt and pepper.

Drain the rice and layer it on top of the chicken and carrots. Using the end of a wooden spoon, poke a few holes in the rice and into them put the whole garlic cloves, then pat the top down with the back of the spoon. Season generously with salt and gently pour over the chicken stock – you are looking for it to cover the top of the rice. Increase the heat and leave the pan uncovered so that the liquid gradually boils away.

When the stock has cooked off, make a few more holes in the rice for the steam to escape then cover the pan with a lid or tight-fitting foil and cook at a low simmer for 5 minutes. Turn off the heat without removing the lid and leave the dish to steam undisturbed for a further 10 minutes. If the rice isn't cooked, add a splash more boiling water and cover again. Let it cool slightly, as you want to serve it warm rather than hot. Remove the garlic cloves, gently spoon the *plov* onto a large dish or platter, keeping the layers, or serve it from the pan. Lastly, scatter over the pomegranate seeds.

Serves 4

250g Basmati rice, rinsed

3 tablespoons sunflower oil

4 carrots, cut into thick matchsticks

4 onions, sliced

1 teaspoon cumin seeds

600g boneless, skinless chicken breasts, cut into bite-sized pieces

½ teaspoon cayenne pepper

4 garlic cloves, unpeeled

360ml chicken stock

Handful of fresh pomegranate seeds

Salt and freshly ground black pepper

Optional additions to scatter on top:

Handful of diced dried apricots, toasted almond slivers, dried sour cherries or barberries

Serves 4

20g butter

100g finely chopped onion

1 garlic clove, crushed to a paste

220g Basmati rice

250g cooked chicken cut into 2cm pieces

500ml hot chicken stock

1 tablespoon extra virgin olive oil

300g coarsely grated courgettes

Pinch of chilli flakes

1 tablespoon chopped coriander

1 level teaspoon Maldon sea salt

Freshly ground black pepper

RICE PILAFF WITH CHICKEN, COURGETTES & CORIANDER

Rory O'Connell

This is what I would call a supper dish, but then I don't really differentiate between supper and dinner as long as the food is delicious. I suppose I connote it with a more informal meal as it arrives at the table in one single dish. This is the type of dish that we all need, as it is a brilliant vehicle for bits of leftover roast chicken, lamb, pheasant or bacon. I pick every scrap off a cooked carcass or bone and that becomes the meat addition to the pilaff. I love the bits of skin, jellied cooking juices and those bits of meat that are trickiest to get it. Invariably the hardest fought for morsels are the sweetest and it just feels great to know you have extracted every bit of value and goodness from the remains of a previous meal.

Apart from the quick cooking of the courgettes in a sauté pan, the rest of the dish happens in just one saucepan. The quantity of the courgette could be increased to make a meat-free dish. In any event it is a delicious and nutritious dish and I find it deeply satisfying and comforting.

———

Melt the butter in a heavy-bottomed saucepan or casserole. When the butter is foaming, add the onion and garlic and stir well. Cover with a piece of greaseproof or parchment paper and the saucepan lid and cook over a very low heat for around 10 minutes. You want the onion to soften without getting any colour.

Add the rice and salt and gently stir through the buttery onions. Allow to cook for 1 minute before adding the chicken and also giving that a gentle mix. Pour in the chicken stock and bring the saucepan to a gentle simmer. Put the lid on and cook over a very gentle heat for about 15 minutes.

Meanwhile, heat the olive oil in a sauté pan. Add the courgettes and season with salt and pepper and a pinch of chilli flakes. Continue cooking over a moderately high heat whilst giving the occasional stir. Remove from the heat when the courgettes are still slightly undercooked.

When the rice has absorbed all of the stock, gently stir in the cooked courgettes and chopped coriander. Taste and adjust the seasoning and serve immediately.

TASTY CHICKEN RISOTTO

Will Greenwood

I grew up in Italy and I played rugby – risotto was always going to be a close personal friend!

———

Heat the butter in a heavy-based saucepan and add the onion and bacon; fry stirring from time to time, until the onion is softened and the bacon cooked. Add the pepper and continue cooking until it is soft – 1–2 minutes. Tip in the rice and stir to make sure it is well coated in the buttery juices. The stock should be brought to the boil in a separate pan and then added to the rice mixture. Bring back to the boil, stirring all the time, then lower the heat and cover with a well-fitting lid. Cook until the liquid has been absorbed and the rice is tender.

Cut the chicken into bite-sized pieces. When the rice is cooked, fold in the chopped chicken and season well with salt and freshly ground black pepper. Then add the cheese, reserving a little to sprinkle on top. Cook for a minute or so until the cheese is melted.

Heap into a large bowl and sprinkle over the parsley and the rest of the cheese. Serve immediately.

Serves 2

25–30g butter

1 large onion, finely chopped

4 rashers of streaky bacon, trimmed and sliced

1 red pepper, deseeded and roughly chopped

225g Arborio rice

600ml homemade chicken stock

225–250g cooked chicken

100g grated cheese (Pecorino/Cheddar mixed)

Handful of flat leaf parsley

Salt and freshly ground black pepper

During the Covid-19 pandemic, 14,610 homeless people across the UK were accommodated in hotels and other forms of housing.

Serves 6

6 large chicken thighs, skin-on, bone-in or 1 chicken, jointed into 8 pieces

2 fat garlic cloves, peeled

2 long sprigs of rosemary

4 rashers of unsmoked streaky bacon

1 onion, roughly chopped

1 carrot, roughly chopped

1 stick of celery, roughly chopped

200ml dry white wine, such as Vernaccia

1 tablespoon tomato purée

1 x 400g tin cannellini beans, rinsed, or 250g cooked beans

500ml hot homemade chicken stock or water

Salt and freshly ground black pepper

CHICKEN 'IN UMIDO' WITH ROSEMARY & CANNELLINI BEANS

Katie & Giancarlo Caldesi

This is a example of Tuscan *cucina povera,* the poor kitchen where flavours are rich but the ingredients are economical. Cooking *'in umido',* in liquid, allows the meat to become so tender that it falls off the bones. Unusually for Italian cooking there is no olive oil in the dish. That is because the fat is from the skin of the chicken and a *'battuto',* which in this case is a paste made from bacon and rosemary. Often recipes that use animal fat are from mountainous areas where olive trees cannot grow. The *battuto* gives a wonderful herby base to the casserole.

The Tuscans are known as the *'mangiafagioli',* the bean-eaters, as beans are so frequently used in their cooking. The humble bean may be known as poor man's protein but the legume family is a combination of carbohydrate and protein and an important part of the Mediterranean diet which is constantly proven to be the healthiest on the planet. Beans are also a good source of fibre and B vitamins, can regulate blood sugar levels and reduce cholesterol.

———

Trim any excess pieces of fat away from the chicken.

Season the chicken with salt and black pepper all over. Heat a large casserole or wide saucepan and brown the chicken, skin side down first, until rich golden brown all over. It will take up to 20 minutes. Let each piece become golden before turning it. Remove the chicken from the pan and pour two-thirds of the fat into a dish; you can use this another day for roast potatoes.

Make a pile of the garlic, rosemary needles and bacon on a chopping board and chop them together with a sharp knife. This is called a *battuto,* a finely chopped mixture, which will melt and form the base of the stew. Fry the paste in the casserole for 5 minutes until it renders down and smells like Tuscany. Add the onion, carrot and celery and cook for 10 minutes. Return the chicken to the pan. Pour in the wine and let the alcohol burn off for 5 minutes then stir in the tomato purée, beans and stock and bring to the boil. Turn the heat down to simmer and leave to cook over a medium heat for 40 minutes or until the chicken is tender and falling off the bone, stirring occasionally.

Give the pan a good shake on the hob; the starch from the beans will thicken the sauce. If it is too watery let it cook for longer. Taste and adjust the seasoning as necessary. Serve with sautéed greens and bread or soft polenta to mop up the juices.

MIZUTAKI NABE

Kimiko Barber

Nabe, or hot-pot, is very popular in Japan where each region, family or even sumo stable has its own favourite recipe using a variety of seasonal and regional ingredients. This recipe is from the Fukuoka prefecture in northern Kyúshú but its popularity has no bounds and is cooked all around Japan. A big communal pot is placed in the middle of the table and diners do their own cooking, choosing a variety of ingredients from a large platter and serving themselves. *Nabe* is easy, tasty, versatile, highly nourishing and above all very friendly. Japanese people know almost instinctively when food is cooked in a pot and ready to eat because they would have been brought up with *nabe* since childhood. So I have adjusted a traditional recipe to suite a non-*nabe*-experienced audience and made it like a hearty stew and all the cooking is done in the kitchen. But to enjoy the spirit of *nabe* I urge you to take the pot to the table and invite your family and friends to serve themselves.

———

Wash the chicken of any trace of blood and put in a large pot with the ginger, green leek tops and rice (any type will do and rice gives the stock a touch of sweetness). Add the water and cover with a lid then bring to the boil over high heat. Remove the lid when it starts boiling (uncovering helps to keep the stock clear) and reduce the heat to low then continue simmering for about an hour, skimming any scum off the surface but and adding water if necessary to ensure the chicken remains covered. If you are using tofu, first drain it by wrapping it in kitchen paper placed on a chopping board and tilt it slightly to let the water run down. Meanwhile prepare the ponzu by mixing all the ingredients together in a non-metallic bowl and set aside.

Strain the stock through a fine mesh sieve – there should be about 1.5 litres. Adjust the taste with salt and pepper and discard the rice and vegetables. Put the chicken aside to cool. Remove the skin and bone and discard, then break the flesh into large bite-sized pieces with your hands.

Put the stock in a large pot, add the chicken with all the vegetables except the watercress/spinach and bring to the boil over a medium heat and cook uncovered for about 5–7 minutes until all the vegetables are cooked through. Remove from the heat, add the watercress/spinach on top, gently stir. Now take the pot to your table and invite everyone to serve themselves with ponzu dipping sauce.

TIP
In Japan *nabe* dinner often ends with adding plain boiled rice into the remaining tasty stock in the pot to make risotto.

Serves 4–6

For the chicken stock:
8–12 chicken thighs, skin-on, bone-in, depending on your appetite

30g piece of unpeeled ginger, scrubbed clean and thinly sliced

2 leeks, green parts only (reserve white parts for the hot-pot below)

Handful of uncooked rice

2 litres water

Salt and freshly ground black pepper to taste

For the hot-pot:
300g firm tofu, drained and diced into large bite-sized chunks (optional)

½ Chinese cabbage, roughly chopped

2 leeks, white parts from above, cut into 2cm thick slices on an angle

2 carrots, peeled and cut into 1cm thick slices on an angle

8 shiitake mushrooms, stems removed

40g watercress or baby spinach

For the ponzu:
60ml soy sauce

60ml mirin

60ml rice vinegar

2 tablespoons freshly squeezed lime juice

Serves 4

2 chicken breasts

200g breadcrumbs

100g Parmesan cheese, finely grated

3 tablespoons curly leaf parsley, finely chopped

2 large garlic cloves, finely chopped

2 medium eggs

4 tablespoons olive oil

Salt and freshly ground black pepper

CHICKEN COTOLETTE

Antonio Orlando

My Sicilian grandmother used to make this for family get-togethers, and then my mother started cooking it for Sunday lunch instead of the usual English roast. Even now when I go back to visit my parents for dinner I'm often greeted by the smell of parsley and garlic as I open the door – this simple dish reminds me of home.

———

Slice each chicken breast horizontally, making 4 fillets in total. Lay the fillets flat, cover with cling film and, using a rolling pin or something similar, roll each fillet until approximately 0.5cm thick. Season to taste.

Mix the breadcrumbs, cheese, parsley and garlic together in a large flat dish. Beat both eggs in another dish. Taking each fillet, dip first into the beaten egg and then coat in the breadcrumb mixture.

Heat the olive oil in a large pan and place each coated chicken fillet into the pan and cook for approximately 3 minutes on each side, until cooked through.

Ideally serve with roast potatoes and *al dente* broccoli.

Paul McConnell - client

Paul McConnell, from Donegal, was married for 38 years when his wife died. He'd lived in Hammersmith for over 40 years and started suffering from depression in 2018. He spent some months in sheltered housing and in a night shelter in Trafalgar Square. Housed in High Barnett, he says he's lonely and the depression just blows up in you. But with help from Janet Sugden at The Passage he's now getting counselling and going to The Listening Place in Pimlico. He also goes to the Maudsley Hospital.

'There's always going to be brick walls there, there's always going to be people there to put you down but I guarantee there's more people there to pick you up.'

JAMAICAN ROAST CHICKEN

Claudette Dawkins

Growing up in a Jamaican household, I had no choice but to be in the kitchen watching my mum cook.

The house was always filled with interesting smells: from her famous rum cakes, curried goat and even sausage and mash, to some not so nice smells like that of 'cow foot', which she used to sometimes cook for my dad!

Saturday was always soup day. Chicken soup, lamb neck soup, red pea soup, fish tea (that's what we called fish soup). You woke up on a Saturday morning and you knew what you were getting for dinner!

Sunday usually meant chicken that was either brown-stewed, curried or baked, served along with rice and peas. Sometimes we would get roast chicken with roast potatoes. This is where the recipe I have chosen comes in. It is my twist on a traditional English roast with influences from my Jamaican background. I took what I learned from my mum and expanded on it. Enjoy!

———

The day before roasting, put all the ingredients into a bowl, except for the chicken, oil, lemon and fresh thyme. Mix well and add enough oil to make a smooth paste.

Place the chicken into a large bowl. Pour the marinade over the chicken and rub well into the chicken, including the cavity.

Put the cut lemon and thyme sprigs into the cavity of the chicken. Cover the bowl with cling film and leave in the fridge overnight to marinate.

Preheat the oven to 160°C/Gas 3. Place the chicken in a roasting tray. Cover the whole tray with foil and seal around the edges of the tray, then put it into the middle of the oven to cook.

After about 1 hour, remove the foil, and turn the oven up to 180°C/Gas 4. Put the chicken back in to brown and finish cooking. After about 30 minutes, check whether the chicken is cooked by inserting a skewer into the thickest part of the thigh; the juices should run clear. If not, return the chicken to the oven and check again after 10 minutes until done.

Once the chicken is cooked, remove it from the roasting tray to a board or serving plate. Allow to rest for about 10 minutes before carving to serve.

Serves 6–8

2 tablespoons natural breadcrumbs

2 teaspoons paprika

1 teaspoon salt

1 teaspoon cracked black pepper

1 teaspoon ground ginger

1 teaspoon garlic powder

1 teaspoon celery salt

1 teaspoon onion granules

1 teaspoon ground allspice

½ teaspoon dried thyme

1 teaspoon sugar

1 medium/large organic chicken

Vegetable oil

1 lemon, cut in half

Few sprigs of fresh thyme

COQ AU VIN

Nour Dakoba

Serves 6-8

1.5kg chicken pieces
(legs, thighs, breast),
skin on

3-4 tablespoons
plain flour, seasoned
with salt and pepper

40g butter

4 rashers of bacon,
chopped

10 spring onions,
trimmed and roughly
chopped

3 garlic cloves,
crushed

250g mushrooms
(portobello, chestnut
or white button), cut in
half

3 tablespoons brandy

250ml red wine

500ml homemade
chicken stock

2 bay leaves

3 tablespoons
tomato purée

3-4 sprigs of flat
leaf parsley

2 tablespoons
thyme leaves

Salt and freshly
ground black pepper

Toss the chicken in the seasoned flour and shake off any excess. Heat the butter in a large pan and brown the chicken all over. Remove and drain on kitchen paper. Add the bacon, spring onions, garlic and mushrooms to the pan. Sauté, stirring frequently, until the onions are lightly browned. Return the chicken, add the brandy and wine and leave to bubble for a couple of minutes to cook off the alcohol. Add the remaining ingredients; cover and simmer for 30–40 minutes.

Transfer the chicken with a slotted spoon to a plate and keep warm. Simmer the sauce until it thickens slightly. Taste, adjust for seasoning, then add the chicken back in. Bring to the boil then serve with steamed new potatoes and green beans.

Nour Dakoba - Chef at The Passage

'The clients can ask me anything they like' is Nour's view; he works more face to face with the clients and knows many of them by name. He has been Claudette's chef for 19 years - she does more on the admin and planning side. He is relaxed, loves a joke and tells volunteers or clients funny things he's heard on the radio that morning. He has good relationships with them individually and appreciates that the group of them will be different at every mealtime.

He learnt to be a chef in his native Kenya and then, in 2000, got the chance to come to the UK. In early 2001 he came to The Passage for a day to cover Claudette's maternity leave; he's stayed ever since. What to cook must be decided on the day, depending on what food has been picked up and brought to the kitchen. He likes to play with fusion food - recently a Korean curry infused with Japanese flavours. His worst nightmares are a volunteer dropping the food, and running out of gas!

Nour's favourite dishes are Cantonese Duck and Chinese Boiled Chicken. He says: 'I lost my family in a very short space of time and my ambition now is to help people.' He likes the balance of helping clients - buttering toast for those with hand injuries or aiding those on crutches with taking their food from the service area to a table. Clients who bin clothes and don't have them washed breaks his heart.

The Passage Kitchen tries to cater to seasons of the year, providing Halal meals and food for Ramadan, those who are vegan or have gluten issues. There are hot winter soups and stews, using fresh vegetables from the Farm in Sussex with whom they work, providing a well-balanced diet for the clients.

'I look forward to coming in the morning; I listen a lot to the clients. It keeps me getting up at 5 o'clock every morning', he says. 'My volunteers are the number one people who have made me what I am now.'

STEAMED THEN CRISP-FRIED DUCK

Shaun Hill

This is a versatile dish, good with salads and a fruity dressing – maybe olive oil, white wine vinegar and a little crème de cassis – in summertime or with root vegetable purées (both celeriac and parsnip work well) in autumn and winter.

The type of duck called for is the Aylesbury or Norfolk variety, both of which are variants on Chinese ducks. One duck will make 4 decent portions and generally weighs about 3kg. Barbary ducks, which are popular in France, will be useless for they are really best treated like steak and served rare; worse the skin is horrible and the whole point of this dish is the crisp, sweet skin. I wrap the ducks in kitchen foil so that the skin is more protected. It becomes fragile as it cooks but the fewer tears and breaks that happen during cooking the better. There is a slight health and safety warning for this dish. The skin is crisp-fried but will be damp from steaming so pat each portion dry with kitchen paper if you want to avoid hot splashes as the duck meets the hot oil.

———————

2 hours ahead:
Lift the neck flap of the duck and cut away the wish bone that forms an arch around the neck cavity. It will be impossible to properly carve the duck with this still in place. Season the bird with salt and pepper then loosely wrap in kitchen foil. If the bird is too large for your steamer then chop off the parson's nose (tail end) as this has no real function in the finished dish.

1¾ hours ahead:
Bring a steamer to the boil on the hob and place the duck gently inside. If you have no steamer, don't despair. Place the wrapped duck on a trivet in a deep roasting tray half filled with water and cover with more foil so that steam rather than oven heat is doing the business.

½ hour ahead:
Carefully lift out the duck and leave for 15 minutes to settle.

¼ hour ahead:
Unwrap the duck and gently divide into sections. Cut away each leg then run a knife along each side of the breastbone to release each breast fillet. Divide each leg into drumstick and thigh and halve each breast. Pat the skin dry.

5 minutes ahead:
Heat a frying pan with 1cm depth vegetable oil, then carefully place each piece of duck, skin side down, into the pan. Do this in 2 or 3 batches. When the skin is crisp and golden lift out onto kitchen paper.

Serves 6

1kg rabbit,
skinned
and jointed

1 medium onion,
chopped

1 medium carrot,
sliced

1 lemon, halved

2 bay leaves

1 Savoy cabbage,
6 good leaves
peeled off

200g caul fat,
cut into 6 pieces

Salt and 1 teaspoon
black peppercorns

*For the wild garlic
yogurt:*
300ml natural yogurt

6 wild garlic leaves
sliced as finely as
possible

Zest and juice of half
a lemon

Salt and freshly ground
black pepper

6 ciabatta rolls
to serve

RABBIT & CABBAGE BURGERS

Oliver Gladwin

Rabbit is such a great meat – lean, flavoursome and low in cholesterol; I don't know why it is so underused and underrated. We have to keep the rabbit population down at the vineyard or they chew the bark off the young vines, so there is often an ample supply.

When I came up with this unusual burger recipe, we were cutting a huge fallen oak tree into a bench to face the view at the top of the farm. I had already prepared some slow-braised rabbit meat but then I had the idea of shaping it into patties, wrapping them in cabbage leaves and cooking them over a smoky barbecue. You will need caul fat in which to wrap the burgers, which protects, seals and moistens the meat. Caul fat, also known as *crépine*, is the very thin layer of fat that separates a pig's stomach and diaphragm – it can be bought from any traditional butcher.

———

Preheat the oven to 160°C/Gas 3.

Put the rabbit pieces in an ovenproof casserole along with the onion, carrot, lemon and bay leaves. Sprinkle in the peppercorns and salt. Add 100ml water, cover with a tight-fitting lid, and put the casserole dish over a moderate heat to bring the liquid to the boil. Then transfer to the oven and braise for 1 hour.

Meanwhile, blanch the Savoy cabbage leaves in boiling water for 2 minutes; drain under cold running water and set aside to cool.

Remove the braised rabbit from the oven and allow it to cool slightly before picking off the meat, discarding any sinew or bones. Put the meat in a mixing bowl with the onion and carrot and moisten with some of the cooking juices. Divide the meat mixture into six portions and squeeze into even-sized patties. Then wrap each one in a cabbage leaf followed by a piece of caul fat.

Light the barbecue or preheat a griddle pan until smoking hot. Grill the rabbit burgers on the barbecue or griddle for 3 minutes on each side. Meanwhile, lightly toast the rolls and make the wild garlic yogurt. Simply stir together the ingredients and season with salt and pepper.

Serve the burgers inside the rolls with a generous dollop of wild garlic yogurt.

TARTIN'FLETTE

Richard Bertinet

There's nothing more comforting than bread, cheese and wine! It's the perfect partnership so, for me, when I'm up in the mountains I love nothing better, after a good day on the slopes, than sitting with friends and family around the table and tucking into some raclette or fondue with some good red. This recipe is as close as you can get to the top-of-the-mountain happiness. It combines everything on a slice of bread. Perfect for breakfast, lunch, an afternoon snack, supper or dinner – anytime really… the wine is up to you! *Bon appétit!*

———

Preheat the oven to 220ºC/Gas 7.

Boil the potatoes in salted water until tender.

Beat the eggs and crème fraîche together in a small bowl. Add the seasoning. Place the slices of bread on a baking tray lined with baking parchment. Put a good tablespoon of the cream mixture on each slice and spread it evenly. Arrange the sliced potatoes on top of the bread, sprinkle over the shallot and add the rest of the creamy mixture.

Divide the Reblochon in four pieces and top the creamy mixture with Reblochon and a rasher of bacon. Bake in the oven until golden on top.

Served with a big green leaf salad and vinaigrette. *Voilà!*

Serves 4

4 small potatoes

2 eggs

200g crème fraîche

4 slices good bread

1 small shallot, finely sliced

1 small Reblochon cheese

4 rashers of smoked streaky bacon

Salt, freshly ground black pepper and a pinch of nutmeg

Serves 2

225g sirloin steak

75g peanuts

1 x 400ml tin coconut milk

For the paste:
1 stalk of lemongrass

Thumb-sized piece of ginger

2 shallots

5 garlic cloves

1 teaspoon dried chilli flakes

1 teaspoon ground coriander

½ teaspoon ground cumin

2 tablespoons fish sauce

2 cardamom pods

1 teaspoon brown sugar

For the coconut rice:
Serves 4
200g Basmati rice

70g butter

50g onion, finely chopped

1 x 400ml tin full-fat coconut milk

200ml full-fat milk

Pinch of salt

To serve:
Few sprigs of fresh coriander

1 lime

1 red chilli

QUICK BEEF MASSAMAN CURRY

Glynn Purnell

I love spices. This super-quick beef massaman curry is packed full of them and is amazingly simple with the coconut rice. You can increase the recipe and make it for a whole load of people, and drop the curry slap bang in the middle of the table with the rice, and people can just dig in. This recipe makes an authentic Thai curry that's ideal for taking the stress out of entertaining guests. It's curry heaven, great for a busy weeknight, but also perfect comfort food.

I find Thai food so satisfying. The sweet/spicy/zesty/creamy combinations are endless. Massaman curry is different from the better-known Thai red or green curries. Massaman is a popular southern Thai curry that's rich and creamy in flavour but relatively mild heat-wise. It contains lots of spices, which can vary from curry to curry, plus meat, sometimes potatoes, peanuts and coconut cream or milk. I absolutely love Massaman – both the beef version and the one I make with chicken.

If you like, you can also double up on making the paste and simply freeze it for another day, and it'll be even quicker to make next time! Job done.

————

Begin by preparing the coconut rice. Preheat the oven to 180°C/Gas 4.

Wash and drain the rice. Melt 40g of the butter in a saucepan until foaming, then fry the onion for 2–3 minutes, or until softened. Add the rice and stir until it is coated in the butter. Tip the rice and onion into a lidded, ovenproof dish.

Bring the coconut milk and milk to the boil in a saucepan, then remove from the heat and pour over the rice. Stir well and season with salt.

Cover with a lid and bake in the oven for 12–15 minutes, or until the rice has absorbed all the liquid and is *al dente*.

Cut up the remaining butter and dot over the rice, then re-cover and leave to melt for a few minutes before fluffing up the grains with a fork.

Make the paste by blending all the paste ingredients together in a small blender. Fry the steak for a couple of minutes on each side. Slice the cooked steak.

Toast off the peanuts in a dry frying pan until nicely browned all over. Sweat the paste off in another pan and add half of the coconut milk. Once combined, add the rest of the coconut milk to the pan. Simmer for 5 minutes and then add the sliced beef and cook for another 2 minutes.

Serve with rice, toasted peanuts and coriander, chilli and lime to garnish.

Serves 4

1 red onion

1 garlic clove

1 lemon

250g mushrooms

2-3 sprigs of
flat leaf parsley

500g fillet steak

1 teaspoon paprika

3-4 tablespoons
olive oil

Knob of unsalted
butter

150ml stock
(or 1 small glass
of brandy)

50ml soured cream

Salt and freshly
ground black pepper

BEEF STROGANOFF

Daniel Katwala

A dish with history and many variations! It is named after the Russian Stroganoff family and is thought to be the invention of their French cooks. One of the earliest references is found in the 1871 edition of Elena Molokhovets's classic Russian cook book, *A Gift to Young Housewives*. The recipe included lightly floured beef cubes (not strips) and a sauce prepared with mustard, broth and soured cream. No onions, no mushrooms, no alcohol. Only 20 years later recipes included onions, tomatoes and a serving of crisp potato straws which are considered a traditional side dish for Beef Stroganoff in Russia.

I was taught this recipe at Westminster Kingsway College, Victoria. It is the one I still use as a base and then vary according to my mood and, probably more importantly, what is in my fridge! Add herbs, tomato, a splash of brandy or white wine – let the recipe be your inspiration!

On my daily journeys to and from college I became acutely aware of the ever-increasing issue of homelessness. I had (and still have) many conversations with those on the streets offering a kind word, a bottle of water, a hot drink.

———

Peel and finely chop the onion and garlic, then finely grate the lemon zest. Clean and tear the mushrooms. Pick and finely chop the parsley.

Place the beef between 2 sheets of cling film. Bash with a rolling pin until 0.5cm thick, then cut into finger-width slices. Mix the paprika, lemon zest, and a pinch of sea salt and black pepper together, and use to dust the beef.

Place a large frying pan over a medium-low heat, fry the onion and garlic in a little oil until softened. Turn up the heat and add the butter and mushrooms, sautéing until the mushrooms are golden brown, then tip onto a plate.

Add a little oil to the pan and fry the beef for 2 minutes, turning, until browned but still pink inside. Stir in the mushroom-onion mixture, add the stock and reduce for 1 minute or until the liquid has almost disappeared.

Remove from the heat and stir in the cream and parsley. Delicious served with bread and gherkins or pasta.

BEEF GOULASH

Nour Dakoba

This is a dish that I sometimes make for our clients, one that I came to around ten years ago. The smoked paprika gives goulash a delicious smoky flavour, particularly if you have smoked paprika to hand. It looks very pretty with the chives chopped into the soured cream.

———

Heat the oil in a large, heavy-based frying pan over a high heat. Season the beef with salt and pepper and add it to the pan, browning it on all sides, then set aside on a plate.

Add the onions to the pan and fry them until lightly coloured, then put in the beef, peppers and paprika and mix all together well. Cover with a lid and cook over a high heat for about 10 minutes, stirring from time to time. Then add the tomatoes, tomato purée, stock and herbs, turn the heat to low and leave to cook, covered, until the meat is tender – this should take around 1½ hours. Check the seasoning and stir through the soured cream.

Serve on large, warmed plates and sprinkle over snipped chives.

Serves 10–12

4 tablespoons olive oil

2kg top quality stewing beef, cut into 5cm cubes

2 large onions, diced

6 peppers, deseeded and diced (use a mix of colours)

4 tablespoons paprika

2 x 400g tins of chopped plum tomatoes

1 x 140g tin tomato purée

850ml homemade beef stock (or use cubes)

Big bunch of flat leaf parsley, thyme and a bay leaf or two

500ml soured cream

Bunch of chives

Salt and freshly ground black pepper

Serves 4

100g puff pastry
(ready-made, but
you can make your
own if you like)

Olive oil

1 onion, diced

2 carrots, diced

250g lean beef mince

1 stock cube

200ml boiling water

1 egg

Salt and freshly
ground black pepper

HOMEMADE BEEF PASTY

Mick Clarke

Home is a precious thing. A house is built with bricks, whereas a home is built with love, laughter, care and memories. This is a recipe I remember my Mum cooking when I was a little boy growing up; true comfort food, great memories and one I cook every now and then for my family. Enjoy!

————

Preheat the oven to 180°C/Gas 4.

Take the puff pastry out of the fridge and allow it to come to room temperature. Heat some oil in a large pan and add the onion, gently frying until turning golden; then toss in the carrots, stirring to mix them in and coat them in the oil.

Add the mince to the pan and brown it all over, seasoning it with salt and pepper. Dissolve the stock cube in the boiling water and pour the stock into the pan. Stir until well mixed and the beef is cooked through (about 10 minutes) and the liquid is absorbed. Check the seasoning and then set aside to cool.

On a well-floured and clean surface, roll out the pastry into 4 thin sheets. Take a dessert-size bowl, place it on the pastry and cut around, setting the circles of pastry to one side.

Spoon the pasty mixture into one half of each circle of pastry, fold the other side over and, with your fingertips, press the edges together to form a sealed pasty.

Crack the egg into a bowl and beat it lightly. Use a pastry brush to brush each pasty with egg. Place the pasties onto a greased baking tray and put into the oven; bake for 20 minutes or until they are nicely browned.

They are delicious eaten hot, with mashed potatoes and vegetables, or cold for lunch the following day.

SPAGHETTI BOLOGNESE (RAGÙ)

HRH The Duke of Cambridge & Nour Dakoba

Nour Dakoba had Prince William chopping carrots on his last visit to The Passage to make a mean version of this Italian classic.

———

First make the sauce. In a large saucepan, heat the oil and butter and fry the onion gently over a medium heat until just softened, then add the carrot and celery and cook for a couple of minutes, stirring. Use a fork to crumble the mince and add that to the pan, stirring to mix all together. Cook until the meat is no longer pink but do not let it brown. Pour in the wine and continue cooking until it has all evaporated. Then turn down the heat and stir in the milk and nutmeg, and cook over a medium heat until the milk has evaporated. Stir through the tomatoes and purée and season to taste with salt and pepper. Simmer very, very gently, uncovered, for about 3 hours, stirring from time to time.

When your sauce is ready, bring a big pot of water to the boil and add a teaspoon of salt. Add the pasta to the water, stir well with a wooden spoon and cook as per the packet instructions. When *al dente*, drain well. Divide the pasta into four bowls and add the hot sauce to each serving, then sprinkle with the parsley and serve the Parmesan in a small dish.

Serves 4

3 tablespoons olive oil

30g butter

1 large onion, finely chopped

1 carrot, scrubbed and chopped

2 sticks of celery, chopped

350g best quality lean beef

250ml dry white wine

120ml milk

Pinch of nutmeg, freshly ground

1 x 400g tin Italian chopped tomatoes

1 teaspoon tomato purée

250g spaghetti or bucatini

50g Parmesan cheese, freshly grated

2 tablespoons freshly chopped flat leaf parsley

Salt and freshly ground black pepper

DIWANI HANDI A POT GONE MAD!

Camellia Panjabi

This is a home-style dish (similar to Lamb Navarin) but used to be served at big banquets in large hotels in Delhi and Mumbai in the 1980s. It is a very contemporary way of eating a tasty curry with lamb and mixed vegetables cooked together. You can use lamb on or off the bone, but I have included stock in the recipe so using stewing lamb or diced shoulder will do nicely.

———————

Wash the lamb in cold water and set it aside. It lightens the colour.

In a deep thick pot, heat the oil and when hot add the cardamom, cinnamon and cloves and simmer over a very low heat to release the spice oils into the cooking oil. Cloves can turn bitter quickly so, within 1 minute, add the sliced onions. Now this is a laborious process, as onions need to be browned and it can take about 12–15 minutes, over a low heat, to result in proper caramelisation.

When the colour of the onions is darkish brown, add the garlic and ginger, followed by the washed lamb (patted dry with kitchen paper) and sauté the lamb in the onions for about 7 minutes, stirring so that all the meat is seared. The lamb will release its juices into the mixture, so let them be re-absorbed to retain flavour.

Add the spices and ground almonds and sauté for 2 minutes, adding a little water so that the spices don't stick to the base of the pan. Now lower the temperature of the heat and pour in the whipped yogurt, stirring continuously. You can put a little water in the yogurt bowl and swill out the little bit of yogurt lodged there. Add the stock and cook the lamb over this low heat until the lamb is 80% done, which should take 20–30 minutes, depending on the age of lamb and size of dice.

Add the tomatoes and salt, stir and simmer for 5 minutes until 90% done. Now, add the vegetables and cook until done. See how much gravy you want and add a little hot water if you prefer. Sprinkle in the garam masala, stir and cook for 2 minutes. Taste and adjust the seasoning.

Best served with white Basmati rice – but also interesting is to cover slices of naan bread on each plate!

Serves 4

500g stewing lamb

5 tablespoons sunflower oil

6 cardamoms

7.5cm cinnamon stick, broken

5 cloves

450g onions, finely chopped

6 garlic cloves, finely chopped

2cm piece of ginger, peeled and chopped

1 tablespoon chilli powder

1 tablespoon ground coriander

½ tablespoon ground turmeric

1 teaspoon ground cumin

5 tablespoons ground almonds

150g Greek yogurt, whipped

700ml lamb or chicken stock

110g chopped tomatoes (tinned will do)

¾ teaspoon salt

400g diced vegetables, a mix of cauliflower, peas, runner beans, peeled potatoes, turnips, carrots – whatever you have

1 teaspoon garam masala

Serves 6

500g boned shoulder
of lamb, trimmed
of fat and cut into
3cm cubes

Plain flour,
for dusting

2 tablespoons extra
virgin olive oil

50g onions, chopped

2 garlic cloves,
finely chopped

225g carrots, diced

1 stick of celery,
finely diced

2 bay leaves

Couple of sprigs of
rosemary

2 x 400g tins chopped
Italian tomatoes

350ml white wine

350ml homemade
lamb stock or water

2 x 400g tins
cannellini beans,
rinsed in cold water
and drained *(see note)

Flaky sea salt
and freshly ground
black pepper

For the gremolata:
4 tablespoons chopped
flat leaf parsley

1 generous teaspoon
grated or finely
chopped organic
lemon zest

2 garlic cloves,
finely chopped

Flaky sea salt,
to taste

SLOW-COOKED LAMB WITH CANNELLINI BEANS, TOMATOES & ROSEMARY

Darina Allen

Bean stews make the perfect one-pot meal – comforting, filling and inexpensive. Gremolata is a fresh-tasting mix of chopped parsley, garlic and lemon zest. I use it to sprinkle over roast or braised meats, pastas or anything pan-grilled – delicious! If you're short of time, you could replace it with some chopped parsley instead.

———————

Dust the cubes of lamb with flour seasoned with salt and pepper. Heat the olive oil in a casserole and fry the lamb in batches until brown. Remove the lamb to a plate and set aside.

Add the onions, garlic, carrots and celery to the casserole and cook over a medium heat for 3–4 minutes until the onions are beginning to soften and are slightly golden. Add the lamb.

Reduce the heat to low and put in the bay leaves, rosemary, tomatoes, white wine and lamb stock or water. Bring slowly to the boil, cover the pan with a lid and simmer very gently for about 1½ hours, or until the lamb is tender. Add the cannellini beans 15 minutes before the end. Remove the rosemary sprigs and bay leaves from the lamb and check the seasoning.

To make the gremolata, mix all of the ingredients in a small bowl, season to taste with salt and serve soon.

Serve, sprinkled with the gremolata.

Note – If time isn't a problem, soak 400g of cannellini beans in lots of water overnight, they will double in volume. Drain, add to the pot with the tomatoes, wine and stock and continue to cook until both the beans and lamb are fully cooked.

MOROCCAN LAMB

Andrew Marr

So far, I have enjoyed a lucky, materially easy life: I have never been homeless. When I was about 18, I did follow an unsuccessful love affair in Spain, by travelling with almost no money. That meant living outside, using town squares and scraps of woodland for overnight sleeping-bag rests, living on tomatoes and bread discarded from bakeries. It was a brief, voluntary adventure only but gave me a tiny insight into how dirty you get very quickly; and how vulnerable genuinely homeless people must feel. Today, I imagine the biggest problem is the lack of physical money. In a world where fewer and fewer people carry change, it must be a lot harder to get the cash you need. My recipe is a made-up one which reflects my enduring love of Middle Eastern food. In the family, we call it Moroccan lamb – apologies, Morocco.

The average leg of lamb weighs 2.25–2.75kg and will feed 8 people.

———

You take a leg of lamb and de-bone it (ask the butcher to do this for you). For the stuffing, which can also be cooked alongside, chop two or three big handfuls of fresh coriander. Dice finely a bag of the darker dried apricots, and the same of dates. Toast a big bag of pine nuts, and then smash them. Dice an onion finely. Combine all the ingredients together with salt and pepper, a little olive oil, and lime or lemon juice. Stuff the lamb. Then, when you have tied it up with string, pierce the skin to insert garlic cloves, and rub the rest with harissa, using quite a lot. Then roast in an oven preheated to 200°C/Gas 6 for 1½ hours and serve, sliced, with couscous and an orange salad. Well, it works for me!

726 homeless people died in England and Wales in 2018, a 22% increase on the previous year.

WED 2ND OCT: LUNCH *WELCOME*
~~~~~
PLEASE NOTE: VOUCHER OR CASH   FREE Bics

PLEASE CLEAR AWAY PLAESTRAYS/PLATES SANDWICH
                                 PRICE BAGUETTE
SOUP: TOMATO INCL MILK FREE
              WHEAT
              CELERY   WRAPS

MAINS: JERK PORK BELLY 40P SALADS
       VEGETABLE STEW 40P CAKES
                             15P YOGHURTS
     POTATO'S CHIPS OR MASHED 15P

       STEAMED BROCCOLI

THE PASSAGE
to ending homelessness

BULGUR WITH LAMB & VEGETABLES

Hussien Dekmak

Bulgur is the grain used in *tabbouleh* and it comes in coarse or fine grades; it's usually durum wheat. It is used extensively in cooking across the Middle East.

———

Put the pieces of meat in a pot, cover with water to a level above the meat and set to boil. Skim the surface of the water using a spoon to remove any scum. Add the bay leaves, cinnamon and cardamom to the meat and let it continue to boil gently. Cook for around 30 minutes or until the lamb is tender. Remove from the heat.

Now prepare the bulgur: put the ghee into a pot and add the chopped onion over a moderate heat and stir until the ghee melts and the onion softens. Add the red and green peppers, stir for 5 minutes then add the bulgur along with some salt and pour the water used from boiling the meat to about 2cm above the level of bulgur in the pot. Add the tomato purée to the bulgur and stir the mixture well. Cover the pot and bring to the boil, then lower the heat and leave it to gently simmer for around 20 minutes. Spoon the bulgur onto a plate and get the pieces of meat and arrange them on top. You can also serve this with a dollop of yogurt.

Serves 4

300g lamb, cut into large pieces

7 bay leaves

3 cinnamon sticks

10 cardamom pods

1 large tablespoon ghee

1 onion, finely chopped

2 red peppers, deseeded and cut in large cubes

1 green pepper, deseeded and cut in large cubes

300g white coarse bulgur

2 tablespoons tomato purée

1-2 tablespoons Greek yogurt (optional)

Salt to taste

The Passage takes its values and ethos from the teachings and example of St Vincent De Paul, a Christian and social reformer, who believed in action rather than words and in hands-on service to vulnerable people. The Passage, as a Vincentian organisation, encompasses a diverse and rich culture and seeks to be a place of hope, aspiration, change and innovation, underpinned by values that reach back over 400 years.

Serves 4

1 large onion,
cut in half
and sliced

3 tablespoons
olive or
sunflower oil

400g minced lamb

1½ teaspoons
ground cinnamon

½ teaspoon
ground allspice

1½ tablespoons
pomegranate molasses
(optional)

200g papardelle

25g flat leaf parsley,
chopped

400g plain
whole-milk yogurt
at room temperature

2 garlic cloves,
crushed

Chilli pepper
to taste

40g butter, melted

Salt and freshly
ground black pepper

PASTA WITH MINCED LAMB & YOGURT SAUCE

Claudia Roden

This interpretation of *manti*, a Turkish meat-stuffed pasta (like large tortellini) with a yogurt sauce, is a deconstruction of one of the most sophisticated and refined of Middle Eastern dishes that was developed in the palaces of Ottoman Sultans in Constantinople – now Istanbul. Here is the story.

The Turks were originally nomadic people from the steppelands of Central Asia on the edge of China who migrated west with their flocks. They started to convert to Islam in the eighth century. As slave soldiers in the armies of the caliphs of Baghdad, they were formidable warriors. By the 11th century they came to form a number of small local dynasties of their own in territories that they captured from the Byzantines as well as in parts of the Arab Empire that were disintegrating. One of these dynasties, the Osmanlis, or Ottomans, captured Constantinople in 1453 and went on to establish one of the most powerful empires ever. The original Ottoman diet consisted mainly of the nomadic staples, yogurt, meat and pasta (*rishte*). The dumplings were adopted from China and the dish was developed perhaps in the Topkapi Palace kitchens.

I have made it in the past – it is a real labour of love. This simple interpretation, using papardelle and a meat sauce, turns it into an easy everyday dish that is just as delicious. My grown-up grandchildren love it.

———

In a large frying pan, fry the onion in the oil over a medium-low heat, stirring often for about 15 minutes, until very soft and lightly coloured.

Add the minced lamb, keep crushing it with a fork and turning it over until it changes colour.

Add salt and pepper, the cinnamon and allspice and the pomegranate molasses, and cook for 5 minutes more. Then add about 150ml water and cook 5 minutes until much of the liquid is absorbed and the meat is very soft.

At the same time cook the papardelle in salted boiling water until *al dente*, drain and pour into a serving dish.

Stir the parsley into the minced meat and mix with the pasta. Beat the yogurt with the garlic and a little salt and pour over the dish.

Mix the chilli pepper with the melted butter and dribble over the top.

ITALIAN SAUSAGE MEAT PASTA

Samantha Cameron

Although I never had a chance to try out this recipe on one of my many visits to The Passage Kitchen, it is a super easy and delicious dish that I often cook at home. It is a favourite of all the family. With thanks to *The River Café Cook Book* by Rose Gray and Ruth Rogers. This is my shortened and simplified version.

————

Fry the red onions in the oil in a large, deep frying pan. Add the meat squeezed from the spicy Italian sausages. Throw in the chopped rosemary and red chilli.

Turn up the heat and break up the sausage meat. Once it's broken up and browned, add a splash of red wine and reduce the heat. Then add the plum tomatoes and stir to amalgamate.

Reduce the sauce, as with Bolognese. Grate loads of Parmesan in a bowl. Once the pasta is ready, mix with the Parmesan, double cream and sauce and serve.

Serves 4

2 red onions, chopped

1 tablespoon olive oil

6 spicy Italian sausages, meat squeezed out and roughly chopped

Handful of rosemary, chopped

1 red chilli, deseeded and diced

Splash of red wine

2 x 400g tins chopped plum tomatoes

Parmesan cheese

200–225g pasta (preferably penne)

300ml double cream

The Passage Vincentian values

'We collaborate across all sectors of society.'

Serves 6-8

1kg belly pork
with the rind scored

6 ripe plum tomatoes,
cut in half

10 garlic cloves,
crushed

2 teaspoons juniper
berries, crushed

2-3 bay leaves

6-8 thyme sprigs

Sea salt and freshly
ground black pepper

SLOW-ROAST PORK BELLY WITH JUNIPER

Jill Norman

Belly pork is quick and easy to prepare and then is left in a low oven to cook for several hours. The refreshing bittersweet taste of juniper marries well with pork; most often used in pâtés and terrines, its sharpness also cuts through the fat of belly pork.

————

Rub a handful of salt over the pork rind and leave the meat in the refrigerator for up to 2 hours. Preheat the oven to 150ºC/Gas 2. Put in a roasting tin just big enough to hold the pork. Let it heat through for a few minutes.

Gently rinse the salt off the pork and dry with kitchen paper. Take out the tin, put in the tomatoes and season them with salt and pepper. Scatter the garlic, juniper berries, bay leaves and thyme over and between them. Put the pork on top, skin side up. Return the tin to the oven and cook slowly for 3–3½ hours.

Heat an overhead grill, take the pork from the oven and put the tin under the grill for 5–6 minutes to crisp the skin. Cover the tin with a piece of foil or a lid and leave to rest for 10 minutes, before lifting out the pork to carve. Scoop up the tomatoes and garlic, leaving behind the fat and flavourings in the pan. Serve the pork with the garlic and tomato 'sauce' and boiled or mashed potatoes.

Montfort House, managed by David O'Sullivan, is a Housing First project with full-time support staff on site 24 hours a day, 7 days a week. With 16 self-contained studio flats, they help very long-term rough sleepers, offering tailored support matched to the individual clients' needs and aspirations. Dean Hajir is one such client.

PEACE.
LOVE.
NOTHING

For the souvlaki:
1 lemon

4 teaspoons dried oregano

1 bay leaf, crushed

2 garlic cloves, peeled

50ml olive oil

600g boneless pork belly strips of pork shoulder, trimmed of excess fat and sinew, cut into 2.5cm cubes

Sea salt and freshly ground black pepper

For the butter beans:
1 fennel bulb (about 300g)

60ml olive oil

2 garlic cloves, crushed with a pinch of sea salt

Pinch of chilli flakes

2 teaspoons fennel seeds

5 medium tomatoes (about 300g) cut into small chunks

2 x 400g tins butter beans

Reserved lemon zest

15g flat leaf parsley

For the tzatziki:
1 teaspoon fennel seeds

1 garlic clove, crushed

250g natural Greek yogurt

Reserved fennel fronds and tops

Pinch of caster sugar

Squeeze of lemon juice

Pinch of sea salt

Lemon wedges, to serve

PORK SOUVLAKI, BUTTER BEANS & FENNEL TZATZIKI

Maria Elia

Trimmed pork belly is the most flavourful for souvlaki as there's just enough fat in the meat to heighten the taste and stop it from drying out, but you could certainly use a leaner cut of pork such as shoulder or loin; belly is my preference! If pork's not your thing, substitute with chicken.

You will need four 23cm metal skewers or four 23cm wooden ones, pre-soaked in water to prevent them from burning.

———————

Remove two strips of zest from the lemon using a potato/vegetable peeler and set aside for the beans.

Put the oregano, bay leaf and garlic in a pestle and mortar, add a large pinch of sea salt and crush to make a paste. Add the olive oil and juice from half the lemon and pour over the diced pork. Refrigerate for at least half an hour or overnight. (If marinating overnight and time permits, remove from the fridge and allow the pork to come to room temperature, as the meat will cook more evenly.)

Preheat a griddle or grill over a medium high heat. Evenly thread pork onto the skewers, season each with sea salt and place on the hot griddle for approximately 4 minutes on each side until thoroughly cooked.

To make the Greek-style butter beans, cut the top and fronds from the fennel and set aside for the tzatziki. Slice the bulb in half lengthways, remove and discard the tough outer layer and thinly slice.

Warm the olive oil in a wide-bottomed pan, add the fennel, garlic, chilli flakes and the fennel seeds and cook over a medium heat for approximately 2 minutes until slightly softened. Stir in the tomatoes and their juices and continue to cook for a further 3 minutes until the tomatoes have softened.

Drain and rinse the beans and add them to the tomatoes with the reserved lemon zest and cook for approximately 5 minutes until the beans are warmed through, then lightly crush the beans using the back of a spoon. Remove the zest, add the parsley and season with sea salt and pepper to taste and serve warm.

To make the fennel tzatziki, put the fennel seeds, garlic and sea salt in a pestle and mortar and crush to make a paste. Transfer to a bowl, mix with the yogurt, fennel, sugar and lemon juice. Season to taste and refrigerate until required.

To serve, divide beans between four plates, top with souvlaki and their juices, add a spoon of tzatziki and a wedge of lemon and serve immediately.

3 tablespoons extra virgin olive oil

2 garlic cloves, peeled and finely grated

300g tomatoes, peeled, deseeded and chopped

1 tablespoon tomato purée

1 tablespoon coriander seeds, freshly ground

6 (about 475g) chorizo-style smoky sausages, skins removed

6 cherry tomatoes, squashed to flatten a little

8 black olives, roughly chopped

4–6 quails' eggs or small hens' eggs

For the coca:
250g strong white flour, plus extra for kneading

2 teaspoons easy-blend dried yeast

Pinch of caster sugar

1 tablespoon extra virgin olive oil

200ml hand-hot water

1 teaspoon sea salt flakes, crushed

To serve:
Natural yogurt, strained through a fine sieve for 15 minutes

SPICY SAUSAGE COCA WITH EGGS & SQUASHED TOMATOES

Linda Tubby

Coca is a Spanish pizza and makes a great base for any number of toppings. Use a soft chorizo-flavoured style sausage for this, not the hard, dried Spanish sort. Or you can use any type of sausage you like, spicy or plain.

————

Start by making the *coca*, sifting the flour into a bowl and mixing in the yeast, sugar and salt. Make a hollow in the centre and pour in the oil and hand-hot water, then mix with your hands until the dough comes away from the sides of the bowl. Add a little more warm water if too dry. Transfer to a lightly floured surface and knead for about 5 minutes until smooth and elastic. Form the dough into a ball and put in an oiled bowl, cover with non-pvc cling film and leave for about an hour until doubled in size.

Meanwhile, make the topping. Heat 1 tablespoon of the extra virgin olive oil in a pan with the garlic over a medium heat. As soon as the garlic sizzles without it browning, stir, add the tomatoes and purée and cook for about 8 minutes until thickened. Remove from the heat and set aside to cool.

Mix the ground coriander into the skinned sausage meat. Heat another tablespoon of the oil in a frying pan and add the meat. Break it up with a fork into small pieces while stir-frying until just firming up. Mix it into the tomato mixture and cool completely.

Preheat the oven 220ºC/Gas 7. Tip the dough onto a lightly floured surface and knead for a few minutes. On a large baking tray roll the dough into a flat rectangle about 25 x 30cm (perfection not required!), pushing out to the edges. Make six evenly spaced hollows on the surface pressing them down so the dough doesn't rise to fill them. Surround the hollows with the cold tomato and sausage mixture. On top of that add the squashed tomatoes and roughly chopped olives. Spoon over the remaining extra virgin olive oil and bake for 6 minutes.

Press down into the hollows again, crack an egg into each and bake for about 12 minutes until the yolks are still soft, the white of the egg just set and the dough risen and golden. Eat right away with the strained yogurt.

SUQUET

José Pizarro

Many years ago, when Catalan fishermen returned to their home shores, they faced the same dilemma that has confounded commercial hunter-gatherers since the beginnings of time. To eat or to sell?

However cold and hungry they were, financial reality must always have meant that the very best and freshest produce had to be sold. But some fish were not exactly beautiful or even the nicest tasting. So developed this 'leftovers' stew – every crew made their own and I expect all thought theirs was the best!

Tasty and quick to prepare, *suquet* is still a great antidote to tiredness and cold. Of course now we can update with tinned tomatoes and ready-made stock – but the essence of the dish remains true to its origins. You do not need to buy the finest fish; just be sure not to overcook it.

It is the *picada* which really makes this dish something special, although in reality I doubt many of those old fishermen actually had dark chocolate to hand.

I like to take a bowl of this on a cold winter evening. The simple but intense flavours provide real warmth inside. Delicious with crusty bread on the side. Enjoy!

————

Heat 75ml of the oil in a large pan, add the onion and gently fry for 15 minutes until softened. Add the garlic and fry for a couple of minutes then add the tomatoes and plenty of seasoning. Simmer gently for 30–45 minutes until really thick but not dry.

Meanwhile, make the *picada*. Heat a little of the oil in a pan and gently fry the garlic and onions until soft. Remove from the pan and set aside. Heat a little more oil and fry the bread until golden but not crunchy. Add to the onions and garlic with the rest of the ingredients and whizz in a blender or mash in a pestle and mortar, with enough of the oil to make a paste. Set aside.

Add the stock to the reduced tomato mixture and bring to a simmer. Insert the tip of a sharp knife into the potatoes and twist to crack them open (instead of slicing). Add to the pan and cook for 15 minutes until starting to soften.

While the potatoes are cooking, heat the remaining oil in a non-stick pan. Dust the fish in flour and fry for 1–2 minutes until lightly golden on both sides. Set aside.

Once the potatoes are nearly cooked, add the *picada* to the sauce and stir well. Nestle the fish into the pan and cook for a further 4–5 minutes until the sauce is thickened and the fish just cooked. Divide between warmed plates and finish with chopped parsley and a splash of extra virgin olive oil.

Serves 6–8

100ml extra virgin olive oil, plus extra to serve

1 large onion, finely chopped

2 garlic cloves, crushed

2 x 400g tins chopped tomatoes

1 litre fresh fish stock

600g new potatoes

600g mix of monkfish, turbot and hake in large pieces

Plain flour to dust

Sea salt and freshly ground black pepper

For the picada:
100ml extra virgin olive oil

2 garlic cloves, crushed

2 small onions, chopped

1 slice white sourdough or other bread

2 squares dark chocolate, grated

20g blanched almonds

Handful of parsley, plus extra to serve

FISH STEW

Nathan Outlaw

For most of us, becoming homeless is something we put to the back of our minds because 'it will never happen to me!'. However, increasingly, homelessness is a situation that faces people from all walks of life on a daily basis and, once there, it's very difficult to find a way back.

When I began working with The Goring Hotel, I was introduced to The Passage, London's largest voluntary sector homeless resource centre, and to the Hotel School. Initially I was sceptical but, having seen the partnership in action and worked alongside some of the people who have come through the School, I have witnessed the transformation that can be achieved as people who thought they had lost everything gain the skills, confidence and self-respect to become valued members of staff in the hospitality sector.

I think everyone deserves a second chance and being a part of this fantastic initiative to offer one to people who, for a variety of reasons, have found themselves literally 'out in the cold' is an honour.

This cookbook, as well as being a great collection of recipes, represents something that most of us take for granted, the ability to cook tasty, nutritious food to enjoy with family and friends in our own homes.

The recipe I have contributed is for my favourite fish stew. It's a recipe made for sharing and gives you a 'foodie hug' when you eat it. Fish is extremely nutritious but it can be an expensive item on the shopping list. However, in this recipe, a little goes a long way so it's a winner all round!

By buying this cook book, you've helped make a difference. So, all that remains is to thank you for your support and to encourage you to try some of the recipes. Enjoy!

Preheat the oven to 180ºC/Gas 4.

Cut the monkfish into 8 equal chunks. Halve each red mullet fillet to give 8 pieces. Put the monkfish, red mullet, prawns and mussels into a bowl and add the garlic, thyme, lemon zest, olive oil and some salt and pepper. Mix carefully then cover and place in the fridge to marinate for 1 hour.

For the stock, line a roasting tray with baking parchment then lay the cod head and reserved fish heads and bones onto it. Place the tray into the oven to roast for 25 minutes. Turn the heads and bones over then roast for another 25 minutes.

Remove the tray from the oven and place over a medium heat on the hob. Add the wine then stir, scraping the tray to deglaze. Simmer for 5 minutes

Serves 8-10

1 monkfish tail, about 1.5kg, trimmed of sinews (bone removed and reserved)

2 red mullet, about 600g each, filleted (heads and bones reserved)

8 large or 16 medium prawns, shelled and cleaned

40 live mussels, de-bearded and rinsed

1 garlic clove, chopped

1 sprig of thyme, leaves picked and chopped

Zest of 1 lemon, finely grated

100ml light olive oil

1 large cod head, cleaned

300ml white wine

Sea salt and freshly ground black pepper

For the stew:
Light olive oil, for frying

2 onions, sliced

4 garlic cloves, crushed

2 fennel bulbs, finely chopped

½ teaspoon dried chilli flakes

Finely grated zest and juice of half an orange

Large pinch of saffron strands

3 bay leaves

1 sprig of thyme

50g tomato purée

2 x 400g tins plum tomatoes

Cont'd

For the spicy anchovy mayonnaise:

2 egg yolks

Pinch of saffron

2 garlic cloves, chopped

1 chilli, deseeded and finely chopped

4 salted anchovies in oil

Juice of half a lemon

Approx. 400ml olive oil

Salt and freshly ground black pepper

To serve:

1 large baguette

Light rapeseed oil for frying

1 garlic clove, halved

then tip everything into a large pot and add water to cover. Bring to the boil, skim off any impurities then lower the heat and simmer for 30 minutes.

Meanwhile, heat another large pan over a medium heat and add a drizzle of olive oil. Once hot, add the onions, garlic and fennel then cook, stirring occasionally, for 5 minutes. Add the chilli flakes, orange zest, saffron, bay and thyme and cook for 2 minutes. Stir in the tomato purée and cook, stirring frequently, for 5 minutes.

Next, add the chopped tomatoes and orange juice then cook for 10 minutes, stirring occasionally. Carefully pour the mixture through a sieve onto the vegetables and simmer the mixture for 20 minutes. Taste and adjust the seasoning if necessary.

Cut the baguette into thin slices. Heat a 1cm-depth of rapeseed oil in a wide pan and, when hot, shallow-fry the bread slices until golden on both sides. Drain the *croûtes* on kitchen paper, rub with the cut surface of the garlic and season with salt. Keep warm.

Add the monkfish to the stew base and cook for 1 minute, then add the red mullet and mussels and cook for another 2 minutes. Finally add the prawns and cook for 1 minute. Before serving, remove any mussels that haven't fully opened and discard.

Serve the stew in the centre of the table with the *croûtes* and spicy anchovy mayonnaise on the side.

Spicy Anchovy Mayonnaise:
Place all the ingredients except the oil into a blender or small food processor and blitz for 1 minute. Add the olive oil very slowly through the funnel until everything is combined and you have a thick mayonnaise. Season the mayonnaise, scrape into a bowl, cover and refrigerate until required.

It costs over £6 million a year to run The Passage, of which only 30% is funded from statutory sources; the rest is raised from voluntary donations, including individuals, corporate partners, schools and churches, charitable trusts, events and legacies. Initiatives such as *A Taste of Home* help to generate vital funds to support their work.

Serves 3-4

*For the curry paste
- dry ingredients:*
1 teaspoon ground turmeric

2 tablespoons
coriander seeds

½ star anise

18 cardamoms

Small pinch of mace

Pinch of grated nutmeg

3 cloves

¼ small cinnamon stick

1 teaspoon palm sugar
(brown will do)

*For the curry paste
- wet ingredients:*
2 tablespoons almonds
or macadamia nuts

1 or 2 whole red bird's eye
chillies, chopped

1 large, mild red chilli,
chopped

10cm piece of ginger,
peeled and sliced

Big bunch of coriander
roots, washed (use the
white parts - the leaves
will get used later)

The weird bits:
1 tablespoon fermented
shrimp paste

475ml coconut milk

110ml Amontillado sherry

JEZZA'S MONKFISH CURRY

Jeremy Goring

This is great for the heads or cheeks of any large round white fish, such as hake or monkfish, but you can make life easier and a bit less messy by substituting an equal amount of monkfish tail, prawns and squid.

The curry paste is the most labour-intensive part although strangely relaxing if executed with a drink and some good music; therefore make double and keep the rest in a jar for up to a week.

————

First prep the seafood: peel and de-vein the prawns, keeping the heads and shells. De-bone the monkfish tail by running a thin-bladed knife along the tailbone on both sides and cut the flesh into man-sized cubes (reserve the bone). De-beak the squid and cut them into hoops. Leave the legs and heads in one piece for gory effect.

Put the prawn meat, squid and monkfish flesh in a bowl and season with about 120ml of coconut milk, plus a glug of fish sauce. Strain.

Then brown the seafood: heat 3 tablespoons of the oil until it is pretty hot in a wok. Add the squid pieces and sear them until they go a little brown and pop (about 1½ minutes on each side for body, 1 minute for the legs). Remove from the wok. Sear the prawns for about 15 seconds per side and remove from the wok. Finally sear the monkfish for about 1 minute per side. You don't want any of these three to be fully cooked through as the job gets finished later. Place them all in a bowl so that the juices that form can be used.

Now make a dead simple fish stock: using the unwashed wok plus its oil, sear and brown off the prawn shells, heads, and diced monkfish bone. Add 2 tablespoons of the diced onion plus 2 crushed garlic cloves. Continue to brown the lot and season lightly with salt and pepper. Then add a glug of the sherry while pan is very hot; this will deglaze (unstick) the delightful juices. Add 500ml of warm water to this and bring to the boil; then lower the heat and let the mixture simmer slowly for 20 minutes. During this process use a potato masher to crush the bones and especially the prawn heads to release their magnificent sweet flavour!

Take off the heat and sieve into another pot using the masher to squash maximum juice out of the bones and heads. While the stock is simmering, here are two jobs:

Job A – wang up some crispy garlic flakes: fry off some thin slices of garlic (cut with the grain, using about 6 big cloves) until golden brown and place on a tissue.

Job B – sort the rice… wash it for about 10 minutes either in a pot by running cold water over it, or in a sieve (less effective). Boil in unsalted water as per instructions until *al dente*. Strain and put in a big bowl; keep warm covered with a damp cloth.

Make the curry paste:
Roast the dry ingredients in a pan for 2 minutes without burning. Crush them to a fine powder in a pestle and mortar (for best results), or cheat and use a spice grinder (a coffee grinder will do). Add the wet ingredients and blend in a blender, pulsing in short bursts to prevent burning out the motor, until smooth.

To make the curry:
Wipe the wok above, and heat some oil in it. Add the shrimp paste and 'roast' for 1 minute to release flavour, then add the plug of coconut cream found in your tin of coconut milk and cook this until it splits (about 10 minutes over a medium heat). Stir in the curry paste and cook for about 15 minutes, keeping it moving! The rest of the onions and 3 crushed garlic cloves go in next; cook for another 5 minutes. You should have a soft, tight, aromatic richly inviting paste on your hands!

Pour in all the fish stock and some of the coconut milk and add the potatoes. Bring to the boil and allow to simmer for 10 minutes. Stir in the aubergine and snake beans and simmer for another 2 minutes. Tip in the rest of the coconut milk to taste, then the fish, sprouts, cucumber and spring onions. Season with fish sauce and add the finishing touches of roughly cut coriander leaves, the garlic flakes and a sprig of basil, using the fish sauce for a final seasoning.

Serve with bowls of rice on the side – you can dip the rice into the curry.

Main ingredients:
1 large onion, finely diced

11 garlic cloves, crushed

70g spuds, peeled and diced large

1 medium Thai pea aubergine, roughly chopped

70g snake beans, cut into 2.5cm lengths

70g cucumber, diced large

Sprinkling of spring onions

Sprinkling of shoots or sprouts

18 tiger prawns, raw, whole

About 500g monkfish tail, on the bone, skinned

4 mid-sized squid, whole, cleaned

4-5 tablespoons grape, rapeseed or olive oil

Finishing touches:
Fish sauce

Garlic flakes (see Job A)

Coriander leaves

Sprig of Thai basil

Thai or Basmati rice

SAM'S ROAST MARINATED SALMON

Sarah Stacey

My home is hugely important to me so I am very glad to be able to contribute in a small way to this book.

I first had this salmon dish at my friend Sam's house in Fremantle, Western Australia and it was so scrumptious I asked for her recipe. It's a side of salmon marinated in a fusion of flavours, laced with honey and baked whole. Over the years I have adapted it in various ways. I used to serve it hot and then I discovered that it's actually more delicious – and easier timing-wise for dinner parties – at room temperature. So usually it is cooked an hour or two beforehand. My husband likes it so much he looks cross if people want seconds so I frequently get a huge side of salmon to cook whole. You can successfully apply the same flavours and principles to salmon fillets, but it doesn't look as impressive.

Quantities are pretty elastic – so you don't need to be precise but I err on the more rather than less side. It is a very kind dish but best avoid over cooking, you want it a bit pink still – although it's always unctuous because of the marinade.

———

You need a roasting tin big enough to take the whole salmon side; you can curve it if needed but it should lie flat. Also, check you have a big serving platter or tray.

At least two hours, and up to a day before if you like, put two large and long pieces of strong foil in the tin, one side to side, the other at right angles so you can make into a parcel when you roast the salmon. This also helps you lift it out of the tin and onto a serving platter once cooked. Now lay the salmon on the foil.

Mix up the marinade and pour over the salmon. Baste it occasionally. I turn the salmon over so the non-skin side lies in the marinade.

When you want to cook it, heat the oven to its highest setting. Turn the salmon skin side up and baste with the marinade again; I usually drizzle on some more runny honey if it's to hand. Pack up the salmon parcel, pleating the edges.

Put the salmon in the oven, reducing the heat to about 200ºC/Gas 6. Allow say 10–12 minutes for a 1kg fish, up to 17–20 minutes for a 2kg one. Timing depends also on the thickness of the fish. You can unwrap it and run a sharp knife down the middle to see if it's cooked to your liking and baste it at the same time. Still wrapped it will go on cooking after you take it out – but don't be tempted to go for more than a few minutes. If it's done to a turn, unwrap and leave to cool a little.

Use the foil to lift it onto a serving platter. Gently pull the foil out. Scatter on spring onions, pepper, coriander etc and serve with the marinade, if you wish. *Voilà*!

Serves 8–10

1kg/2kg side sustainably produced salmon, boned but skin on; I reckon 2kg for 8–10 guests with leftovers

For the marinade:
Small/medium bottle of dark soy sauce

Several garlic cloves, minced

Big chunk of ginger, grated

About half a small jar of runny honey

Big bunch of coriander, leaves stripped and stalks chopped very finely

2–4 stalks of lemongrass, bashed

To serve:
Bunch of spring onions, finely sliced

Chopped red peppers and/or pomegranate seeds

Coriander leaves

Sliced cucumber (if you like)

Lime quarters (one per person)

For the sauce:
Generous handful
of spinach

100g feta cheese

240ml coconut milk

1 tablespoon cornflour

For the rice:
450g long-grain rice

1 tablespoon olive oil

3 spring onions,
chopped

2 garlic cloves,
finely chopped

250ml vegetable stock

15g basil leaves

475ml water

For the salmon:
4 salmon fillets,
approx. 250g each

4 tablespoons cucumber
and mint dressing

60g dill fronds
to taste

Salt and freshly ground
black pepper to taste

**For the cucumber
and mint dressing:**
½ cup mint leaves

2 garlic cloves

2 cucumbers, sliced
in half and the seeds
scooped out and
discarded

Juice of half a lemon

500g natural
yogurt

Olives to serve

CRIOLA SALMON

Nancy Almeida

I grew up in Sweden and my parents come from a West African island. But for most of my adult life I've lived in England so I have lots of mixed influences. A few years ago, I fell very ill and depressed and started needing to push myself to see the beauty of the world and to be more healthy.

Today I'm increasingly conscious about a more positive lifestyle because things can affect one's wellbeing so much. I started to take pictures on my walks and would post them online just in case someone else needed to see something pretty to motivate them that day.

And then I started cooking because I wanted to have an all-round positive lifestyle. There's a saying in Swedish – *ögat ska ha sitt,* meaning 'the eyes need to be fed as well'. And I totally agree with that, and it's what I try to do!

———

Preheat the oven to 180ºC/Gas 4.

Start by making the sauce. Add the spinach, cheese and milk to a blender (a smoothie blender will do) and blend to a liquid. Pour it into a saucepan and cook over a low heat, stirring frequently. When the sauce starts to boil, add the cornflour and stir vigorously, removing any lumps with a smaller spoon, until it reaches a creamy consistency. Cover and keep warm.

Soak the rice in cold water for 5 minutes before cooking. Heat the olive oil in a medium-sized saucepan, fry the spring onions, garlic, basil and vegetable stock over a gentle heat to produce a green marinade. Pour in the measured water, bring to the boil, then add the drained rice. Stir evenly and cook over a very gentle heat, covered, until tender and the liquid has evaporated.

Then tackle the salmon; make a simple cucumber and mint dressing made by blending the mint leaves, garlic, cucumbers and lemon juice together in a food processor until very fine. Empty into a bowl and stir in the yogurt.

Place the salmon on a baking tray, coat in the mixture and sprinkle the dill over the top of the fillets. Season with salt to taste. Put the tray in the preheated oven and bake for 15 minutes.

Serve the salmon on a platter with the rice on the side. Pour the green sauce over the fish to finish and decorate by adding a couple of big olives on the side.

GRILLED SARDINES WITH A TOMATO, GARLIC & THYME DRESSING

Rick Stein

I wrote this recipe as a result of some irritation at being given such delicacies as perfectly fresh sardines in the fishing village of Port-Vendres that had been fried within an inch of their lives. It was almost like eating sticks. I'd noticed the same phenomenon after a morning's freshwater fishing on the Dordogne River. We had a lunch of hard-fried gudgeons, minnows, crayfish and eels, all overcooked in the same way; the saving grace was the mayonnaise. Granted a lot of river fish are quite tasteless but not sardines. No excuse there. Here's a better way.

———————

Mix the ingredients for the dressing in a small bowl and season with salt and plenty of pepper.

Brush the sardines all over with the oil and sprinkle them with a pinch of salt. Grill them on a hot barbecue or under a hot grill for about 2–4 minutes on each side, depending on size.

Spoon the dressing over and around the sardines and serve with a green salad.

Recipe taken from Rick Stein's Secret France *(BBC Books, £26)*

Serves 3–4

12 sardines, cleaned

1 tablespoon olive oil

For the dressing:
Zest and juice of half a lemon

2 tablespoons extra virgin olive oil

½ large garlic clove, grated or very finely chopped

¼ teaspoon piment d'Espelette or a pinch of chilli flakes

1 medium tomato, skinned and cut into a small dice

1 small shallot, finely chopped

1 thyme sprig, leaves chopped

1 teaspoon chopped flat leaf parsley

Salt and freshly ground black pepper

SEARED COD WITH MUSSELS & CAVOLO NERO

Emily Watkins

The sweetness from the apples in the cider in this sauce marries so well with the cod and mussels. But the beautiful earthy cavolo nero balances the whole dish. It was so popular at the Kingham Plough that it was on the menu time and time again. If cod is unavailable hake or haddock would work really well too.

———

Prepare the cavolo nero by stripping the leaves off the stems and washing.

Put the cream in a saucepan, bring to the boil and reduce it by half. Set aside.

Place a heavy-based frying pan over a medium high heat and add a couple of tablespoons of cooking oil. Season the cod then place, skin side down, in the hot oil, holding each piece firmly to stop it curling. Cook until the edges are golden. Use a spatula to carefully turn the fish over and cook for a minute. Lift out the cod and set aside. Turn up the heat, add the mussels, then pour in the cider. Cook until all the mussels are open. Scoop them out and place in a bowl. Stir the cream into the cider and bring to the boil. Place the cod back in the pan and immediately turn off the heat, allowing the cod to gently finish cooking in the sauce.

Cook the cavolo nero in seasoned boiling water for about 3 minutes until tender. Drain off and finish with a good quality cold pressed oil, salt and pepper.

Take the mussels out of the shells and add back into the sauce, together with the chopped parsley. Serve with the cavolo nero and lemon for squeezing.

Serves 4

500g cavolo nero

300ml double cream

2 tablespoons olive oil

4 cod fillet portions

500g mussels (washed and de-bearded)

200ml dry cider

Cold-pressed oil, for drizzling

Handful of parsley, finely chopped

Lemon for squeezing

Sea salt and freshly ground black pepper

Valentin Anita - client

A native Romanian, Valentin Anita was married for 20 years and divorced five years ago. After spending six months homeless in Germany, he got a four-day mini job and used the money he earned to buy a ticket to London on 28 November 2019. Ten days later he did his first work, part-time street cleaning at night for Westminster Council and for Veolia as an agency worker. Bed was a sleeping bag in a work shelter. The job came to an end in March 2020 and he came to The Passage, seeking help to get back on his feet. He is now well on the way.

Serve 2

200g shiitake
mushrooms, whole

1 tablespoon cornflour

2 tablespoon rapeseed oil

1 plump garlic clove, peeled
and crushed

1 red chilli, deseeded
and finely chopped

2 tablespoons
rice wine

1 teaspoon Chiu Chow
chilli oil

250g cooked egg noodles
medium thick (or noodles
of your choice), lightly
dressed in toasted
sesame oil

Large handful of fresh
raw beansprouts, washed

2 tablespoons
light soy sauce

For the marinade:
1 tablespoon peeled and
grated ginger

1 teaspoon organic
miso paste

1 teaspoon dark soy sauce

2 tablespoons good
quality runny honey

To serve:
Handful of pine nuts,
toasted

2 spring onions, chopped,
sliced on a deep angle
(horse-ear shaped), or
into rounds

CHING'S SPICY SWEET MUSHROOM CHOW MEIN

Ching-he Huang

This is an all-round Asian Fusion dish – the miso, soy and honey works so well. A real mix of umami: the dish is salty, spicy, pungent, sweet and nutty (all the notes of Chinese cooking). It is perfect with a glass of Sancerre or your favourite white wine.

———

Put all the ingredients for the marinade Into a bowl and mix well to form a paste. Add the mushrooms and marinate them for 5 minutes.

Just before wokking, dust the marinated mushrooms with cornflour.

Heat a wok or pan over high heat and add the rapeseed oil. Toss in the garlic and chilli and cook, stirring for a few seconds to release their aroma. Add the marinated mushrooms and wok, tossing for 1 minute and, as they start to caramelise, add the rice wine, 1 teaspoon Chiu Chow chilli oil and toss, cooking for 10 seconds.

Add the cooked egg noodles and beansprouts and toss through well. Season with light soy sauce to taste and more Chiu Chow chilli oil if you like spice.

Sprinkle in the toasted pine nuts and spring onions, spoon out onto two plates and serve immediately.

Serves 4

60g salted butter

4 tablespoons
olive oil

1 tablespoon
fresh rosemary leaves

600g mixed wild
mushrooms, cleaned
and roughly sliced

2 garlic cloves,
thinly sliced

100ml dry white wine

500ml double cream

2 large handfuls
of spinach leaves,
washed

400g fettuccine

30g Pecorino cheese,
freshly grated

Fine salt and
½ teaspoon freshly
ground black pepper

FETTUCCINE WITH MUSHROOMS, ROSEMARY & SPINACH

Gino D'Acampo

Fettuccine means '*little ribbons*' in Italian and they are somewhat thinner than tagliatelle. Typical of the Roman and Tuscan areas of Italy, fettuccine is one of my favourite pastas. Pecorino is a hard sheep's milk cheese and the better quality you can buy the better your dish will be; most pecorino now is produced in Sardinia.

———

Fill a large saucepan with 4 litres of water, add 1 tablespoon of fine salt and bring to the boil over a high heat.

Meanwhile, place a large frying pan or a wok over a high heat and add the butter, olive oil and rosemary leaves. Add in the mushrooms with 1 teaspoon of salt and fry for 5 minutes, stirring occasionally with a wooden spoon. Add in the garlic and continue to fry for a further 8 minutes. Pour over the wine and bring to the boil for 2 minutes. Lower the heat to medium and stir in the cream with the spinach and pepper to taste. Cook for a further 5 minutes, stirring occasionally.

Cook the pasta in the boiling water until *al dente*. To get the *al dente* perfect bite, cook the pasta for 1 minute less than instructed on the packet and always cook it with the lid off. Stir every minute or so.

Drain then tip the pasta back into the saucepan. Pour over the mushrooms and spinach sauce and stir all together for 20 seconds allowing the flavours to combine.

Serve on warm plates and sprinkle over the Pecorino cheese.

PAN-FRIED BARLEY PASTA, WITH SEASONAL SALAD

Yohanis Gebreyesus

On a clean work surface, mound the beso flour and make a well. Add the water and begin mixing the flour on the side. Gradually incorporate it all into a single ball. Dust with the wheat flour and knead patiently until the dough is supple. Cover the dough with a cloth and set aside to rest for 30 minutes at room temperature.

Roll the rested dough into four cylinders. Then, one at a time, keep rolling until the cylinders are 1cm thick. Cut the rolls into pieces 3.5cm long and place each piece on a pasta board. Using your index and middle fingers, roll each piece of dough along the board, pressing as you go. This creates a hollow from your fingertips on one side and a decorative embossed pattern on the other.

Drop the patterned pasta in boiling, salted water until they start to float. Remove and place in iced water, then drain.

Place a frying pan over a high heat, add the sunflower oil, butter and sage. When foamy add the drained pasta and cook over a medium-high heat until golden brown. Put the pasta on kitchen paper and leave it to cool.

In a small bowl, whisk together the ingredients for the vinaigrette.

Dice all the vegetables, put in a large mixing bowl then add the pan-fried pasta. Pour over the yogurt vinaigrette and toss to combine. Serve cold.

Serves 4-6

125g beso (toasted barley flour)

240ml water

25g wheat flour

1 tablespoon sunflower oil

20g butter

2 sprigs of sage

2 avocados

8 curly salad leaves

160g cherry tomatoes

65g yellow onion

For the vinaigrette:
3 tablespoons olive oil

1 tablespoon red wine vinegar

Juice of half a lemon

1 teaspoon mitmita or cayenne pepper

15g chives, finely chopped

275g natural yogurt

Salt and freshly ground black pepper

Debbie Lee - client

A bubbly, articulate, qualified theatre sister with a good education in Zimbabwe, Debbie Lee came to England in April 2019 ostensibly to care for the elderly through an agency which matched clients with carers. She was paired with a bad stroke victim, who required much lifting with equipment with which she wasn't familiar. For two months she was terrified of screwing up the care of her client and ended up giving notice and sleeping on the street for a night while looking for work.

She heard of The Passage and went there; Fergus Johnston put her in touch with The Marylebone Project, which is helping to get her into her own accommodation and also a job. Being a nurse, she's never done drugs or alcohol. She's the mother of twin boys and a girl, now living in Johannesburg.

Serves 4

3 tablespoons
vegetable oil

1 teaspoon
black mustard seeds

1 teaspoon
cumin seeds

3 garlic cloves,
crushed

2 large potatoes,
peeled and cut into
thick batons

1 teaspoon
chilli powder

1 large onion,
thinly sliced

2 teaspoons
ginger-garlic paste

2 fresh green chillies,
minced

1 teaspoon
ground turmeric

1 teaspoon
garam masala

200g Basmati rice,
washed and drained

Handful of coriander
leaves, chopped

Salt

SPICY POTATO TAHIRI

Monisha Bharadwaj

This simple rice dish is hearty and delicious at the same time. A tahiri is considered to be a vegetarian biriyani – a north Indian hero dish that has meat or chicken, spices and herbs and is often a part of a feast or special meal. Biryani came to India from Persia through the Mughals, an Islamic dynasty that would rule over a large part of India for centuries. As the cuisine developed and spread, some cooks thought that there was great skill in creating a meatless rice dish that could equal the fragrance and glamour of the biriyani. It would be rich with the perfume of the rice and the nourishment of the vegetables. It can be made with any mix of firm vegetables; I've used potatoes in this recipe.

The tahiri must be fluffy – in fact cooks in the imperial kitchens were said to have prepared the rice so perfectly that it resembled diamonds and crystals – so make sure to buy mature Basmati rice which will cook without becoming too starchy. Rice is matured in controlled conditions to regulate moisture, light and air for up to two years so that the outside of each grain dries and locks in the starch. Mature or aged rice is more expensive than new rice so the price will be an indication if the packaging does not mention that it is old.

———

Heat half the oil in a shallow, non-stick frying pan over a high heat, add the mustard seeds and fry until they begin to pop. Add the cumin seeds, then – almost immediately – add the garlic and fry for a few seconds until it turns golden, then add the potatoes. Season with salt, reduce the heat, cover and fry for 15–20 minutes until the potatoes are tender. Stir from time to time to prevent them from sticking. Add the chilli powder when the potatoes are nearly cooked.

Heat the remaining oil in a saucepan, add the onion and fry for 5–6 minutes, stirring intermittently, until browned. Add the ginger-garlic paste, chillies, turmeric and garam masala and fry for 1 minute. Add the rice, fry for 1 minute more, then pour in double the volume of water to the rice. Bring to the boil, then reduce the heat to low, stir once, cover and simmer for 10 minutes until the water has been absorbed and the rice is cooked. Remove from the heat, set aside for 5 minutes, covered, then remove the lid and fluff up the rice.

Gently fold in most of the fried potatoes. Top the rice with rest of the potatoes, sprinkle with the coriander and serve hot.

SWEET POTATO, LENTIL & BASIL BAKE

Chantelle Nicholson

This nourishing dish is packed full of plant-based protein from the lentils and tofu. It works well in both winter and summer and uses a few of my store-cupboard essentials such as tomato purée, lentils and smoked paprika. It is also delicious with other vegetables added in, such as Swiss chard, kale or broccoli.

———

Preheat the oven to 180°C/Gas 4.

For the sweet potato bake, heat the vegetable oil in a casserole dish over a moderate heat. When hot, add the onions, seasoning well. Cook until soft then add the garlic and cook for a further 3 minutes. Stir in the smoked paprika, followed by the tomato purée. Cook for 1 minute then mix in the tomato juice and vegetable stock. Season with salt and pepper and bring to the boil. Add the sweet potato and lentils and mix well. Cover the casserole with a lid, or foil, and place in the oven for 25 minutes, stirring after 10 minutes. Remove from the oven and stir through the basil leaves.

To make the tofu purée, place the ingredients in a blender and blend until smooth. Season with salt and pepper.

Dollop over the sweet potato bake and top with the breadcrumbs and olive oil.

Turn the oven to the grill setting and, when hot, place the bake under the grill for 5–10 minutes until golden brown. Serve with a simple salad or green vegetables.

Serves 6–8

2 tablespoons vegetable oil

2 onions, finely sliced

1 garlic clove, crushed

1 teaspoon sweet smoked paprika

2 tablespoons tomato purée

250ml tomato juice

650ml vegetable stock

1 large sweet potato, washed and grated

250g Puy lentils

Bunch of basil

100g breadcrumbs

2 tablespoons olive oil

Sea salt and freshly ground black pepper

For the tofu purée:
1 packet firm tofu (280–300g)

1 teaspoon nutritional yeast

2 tablespoons tahini

2 tablespoons soy sauce or tamari

Serves 6-8

700g Crown Prince, kombocha or butternut squash, peeled, deseeded and cut into 3cm chunks

400g celeriac, peeled and cut into 3cm chunks

400g parsnips, peeled and cut into 3cm chunks

6 tablespoons olive or rapeseed oil

2 chipotle chillies, deseeded and opened like a book

1 ancho chilli, deseeded and opened like a book

2 onions, chopped

3 garlic cloves, roughly chopped

2 teaspoons ground cumin

1 teaspoon ground coriander

1 teaspoon ground cinnamon

1 heaped teaspoon dried oregano, preferably Mexican

2 tins black beans, rinsed

2 x 400g tins plum tomatoes

1-2 tablespoons soft brown sugar, to taste

30g dark chocolate, at least 70% solids, grated

Small bunch of coriander, leaves picked

To serve:
Guacamole (see page 54)

Soured cream

Rice

MEATLESS CHILLI WITH ROASTED ROOTS & BLACK BEANS

Thomasina Miers

This recipe is rich, warming and incredibly economical, relying on the wonderfully diverse flavours of root vegetables that proliferate the markets in the autumn and winter. You can put as many different roots into this chilli: carrots, beetroots and swede work beautifully, just as you can add minced pork and/or beef if you feel you need a meat fix. The chillies give it a gentle, background heat, whilst the spices add layers of flavour. For a party, serve the chilli with roast or fresh salsas, guacamole, slaw, tortillas and rice; for a mid-week dinner you could just strip it back to soured cream and rice. However many people you are feeding it is a really fun recipe to eat with people you love.

———————

Preheat the oven to 220ºC/Gas 7. Put the squash, celeriac and parsnips on a baking tray, drizzle with half the oil and season generously. Toss everything together with your hands, spread out and roast in the oven for 30–35 minutes until the veg are tender but crisp and golden on the edges.

Toast the dried chilli pieces in a small, dry frying pan for a minute on both sides and then cover with boiling water and set aside. Meanwhile, pour the remaining oil into a large saucepan, add the onions and sweat over a medium heat for 10 minutes until beginning to soften. Season generously, add the garlic and cook for another 5–7 minutes. Drain the dried chillies, finely chop with a knife and add half to the onions with the spices and oregano. Fry for a minute and add the beans, tomatoes, sugar and chocolate, then fill up the tomato tin with hot water and add to the pan.

Bring to the boil, then simmer gently for 15 minutes until reduced. Stir in the roasted vegetables and check the taste. If you want more spice add the rest of the chillies (I usually do!). Simmer for another 15 minutes until the sauce has thickened. Check the seasoning, then sprinkle with coriander and serve with as many delicious salsas and side dishes as you can muster.

The Passage, housed in St Vincent's Centre, aims to help individuals address the issues that have contributed to them being – or are keeping them – homeless, and to enable them to move on to live safe, happy and fulfilling lives.

St VINCENT'S CENTRE

CHILEAN BEAN-POT

Elisabeth Luard

A winter dish from the Chilean highlands, this is a one-pot vegetarian dish of floury butter beans cooked with potatoes and squash enriched with olive oil. You can, if you wish, replace Chile's native bean with any of the multi-coloured members of the haricot family – black, red, white, brown, speckled – which provided the inhabitants of tropical America with their daily dose of carbohydrates, protein, vitamins, minerals and fibre. Fresh corn kernels can be included in season, and you can add a little more protein with a finishing sprinkle of crumbled salty white cheese – feta or similar – or quartered hard-boiled eggs.

————

Drain the soaked beans and bring them to a gentle bubble in a roomy saucepan with enough water to cover generously. Meanwhile toast the garlic bulb on the end of a knife in a flame till the papery skin singes and blackens a little, and add it to the pot. Add the peppercorns (no salt) and 2 tablespoons of the olive oil. Turn down the heat, cover with a lid and leave to simmer gently for 1 hour if the beans are freshly dried (they'll yield a little when squeezed), 2 hours if the beans are hard.

Cook the beans until soft but not yet collapsed, adding a splash of boiling water as necessary. Stir in the squash chunks and bubble up. Add the diced potato, bubble up again, then turn down the heat and allow 10 minutes for the potato to soften. Stir in the shredded greens. Reheat and allow another 5 minutes to cook the greens.

Squeeze the soft contents of the garlic bulb into the broth, discarding the skins. Add the rest of the olive oil and bubble up again to thicken the broth: the oiliness will disappear like magic. Taste and add salt. Ladle into bowls and sprinkle with finely chopped celery leaves and the optional finishing ingredients.

Serves 4–6

350g dried butter beans, soaked overnight

1 whole garlic bulb

4 tablespoons olive oil

About 500g butternut squash, peeled, deseeded and cut into large chunks

1 large potato, scrubbed and diced

2–3 sticks of celery, diced (save the leafy greens for finishing)

750g shredded greens – chard leaves, spinach, spring greens

Salt and ½ teaspoon peppercorns, crushed

To finish (optional):
Green chilli, diced

Coriander leaves

Spring onion, chopped

Serves 4-6

1kg potatoes, peeled

500ml full-fat milk

1 large garlic clove, halved

2 large or 3 small eggs

250g strongly flavoured cheese, grated. Use half for the milk sauce and keep half for the topping.

Salt and freshly ground black pepper

GRATIN DAUPHINOIS

Gyles Brandreth

I am definitely not a skilled cook and this *'recipe'* is really just a guide which you can adapt according to your own taste and what ingredients you have available. It is great for using up leftovers. Use any type of potatoes or cheese. Maybe go wild and mix two types of cheese for the milk sauce! But stick to a standard hard cheese like Cheddar or Red Leicester for the topping.

———

Preheat the oven to 180°C/Gas 4.

Cut the potatoes into rounds about 1.25cm thick. Put them in a pan and add enough well-seasoned milk to cover them completely. Bring the milk gently to the boil then turn down the heat and let the potatoes simmer until cooked but still firm (around 6–8 minutes).

Rub a large cut piece of garlic generously around a wide, shallow, ovenproof dish.

Beat together the eggs with the grated cheese.

Gradually add about around 500ml of the hot milk to the egg and cheese mixture.

Place the par-cooked potatoes into the ovenproof dish and pour the milk, egg and cheese mixture over them. Ensure the mixture covers the potatoes, adding a little more milk if necessary. Adjust the seasoning to taste. Top with a generous layer of grated cheese.

Brown in the oven for around 30–35 minutes until the potatoes are completely cooked and the cheese topping is melted and starting to crisp.

Serve as a supper dish with green salad or green beans or as a side vegetable with fish or meat.

DESSERTS

Dame Louise Casey, Government Adviser to help tackle homelessness

'For forty years The Passage has provided accommodation, support and hot meals for the homeless. The spirit and warmth of what they do is represented in this wonderful book. Buying it will bring a bit of that love to your kitchen and help one more person towards a home of their own too.'

BAKEWELL PUDDING

Shaun Hill

Bakewell tart is evidently known as Bakewell pudding in the Derbyshire town of Bakewell so call it what you will. Cooks know the base mixture by its French name of frangipane in any case. Stone fruits – like cherries, apricots and plums – work particularly well with this, either placed on top of the mixture or served as compôte alongside.

   The pastry for this recipe is not baked blind. However, it is made and rolled the day before and then frozen, so the dish needs to be thought of at least 24 hours ahead.

————

24 hours in advance:
Make the pastry. Sieve together the dry ingredients. Rub in the butter then mix in the egg yolks to form a dough. Roll out the pastry and line a 21cm tart case. Freeze until the next day.

1 hour in advance:
Take the pastry case from the freezer.
Make the Bakewell by creaming together the butter and sugar. Slowly beat in the eggs, then fold in the ground almonds.

Spread the jam across the pastry base and spoon in the almond filling. Smooth the surface then scatter across the flaked almonds.

45 minutes in advance:
Bake the tart for 45 minutes at 180°C/160°C fan/Gas 4.

Serves 6-8

For the pastry:
450g plain flour

100g caster sugar

350g unsalted butter, softened but not melted

2 egg yolks

For the Bakewell/ frangipane:
300g unsalted butter

300g caster sugar

5 eggs

250g ground almonds

½ jar quality raspberry jam

100g flaked almonds

Serves 4

50g cocoa

6 tablespoons
boiling water

3 eggs

4 tablespoons milk

175g self-raising
flour

1 level teaspoon
baking powder

100g baking spread
or soft butter

300g natural caster
sugar

*For the icing
and filling:*
150g Bournville
chocolate, broken
into small pieces

150ml pouring
double cream

3 tablespoons
apricot jam

A little icing sugar

VERY BEST CHOCOLATE CAKE

Mary Berry

A cake made in the processor or mixing machine and therefore very easy – a deliciously naughty icing too!

―――――

Preheat the oven to 180ºC/160ºC fan/Gas 4.

Grease two 20cm sandwich tins and base-line with baking parchment.

First measure the cocoa and boiling water into a large bowl and mix well to make a paste. Add the remaining ingredients and beat again until combined. This can also be made in a processor but be careful not to overwhisk. Divide the cake mixture between the prepared tins. Bake in the preheated oven for about 25–30 minutes until well risen and shrinking away from the sides of the tin.

For the icing and filling, measure the chocolate and cream together in a bowl and sit the bowl over a pan of simmering water for about 10 minutes until melted, stirring from time to time. Set aside and allow to become cold and almost set.

When baked, remove the cakes, turn out onto a wire rack and allow to cool completely. Spread the tops of each cake with apricot jam. Sandwich the cakes with half the icing and spread the remainder on top. Take a small palette knife and draw large 'S' shapes to give a swirl effect – dust with icing sugar and enjoy!

BRAMBLE BUTTERSCOTCH BROWNIE CAKE

paul.a.young

Autumn is my favourite time of year for baking heart-warming comforting chocolate cakes. The seasonal berries, orchard and stone fruits are in abundance and made to be muddled together with rich moist chocolate. A soft, fudgy-centred cake made with 72% Venezuelan chocolate, but you can simply use your favourite variety. Special note – don't worry as this cake drops slightly in the middle. It can be served warm but is best at room temperature.

———————

To make the cake:
Preheat the oven to 180°C/160°C fan/Gas 4. Line a 20cm cake tin with a double layer of baking parchment around the sides and a single disc on the base.

In a saucepan melt the butter, sugar, black pepper, salt and golden syrup until smooth and bubbling. Add the chocolate off the heat and stir well until fully melted. Allow to cool.

Whisk the eggs and strain through a sieve onto the chocolate batter. Mix well until fully incorporated. Now add the flour in one go, mixing very well until fully incorporated.

Pour the batter into the tin, then scatter the brambles across the top. Bake for 1 hour and 45 minutes until the cake has set but is still moist in the centre. It will look slightly underdone but the residual heat will set the chocolate and make the cake very moist.

Allow to cool thoroughly, remove from the tin and place on your cake stand.

To make the bramble butterscotch:
In a medium saucepan melt the butter, sugar and salt together and simmer for 5 minutes stirring occasionally. Take off the heat and add the double cream, standing back as it can splutter. Whisk in well.

Now add the brambles stirring well so they begin to burst and colour the caramel an intense purple and finally stir in the chocolate until melted. Spoon over the cake so it spills down the sides, piling the brambles on the top.

This cake keeps superbly well in an airtight container for a week in the fridge but remember to serve at room temperate to experience all the warming and fruity flavours.

Serves 8

100g unsalted butter

175g light Muscovado sugar

½ teaspoon freshly ground black pepper

½ teaspoon Maldon sea salt

50g golden syrup

165g 72% Venezuelan chocolate, roughly broken

3 medium free-range eggs

50g plain flour

100g brambles/ blackberries

For the bramble butterscotch:
100g butter

100g light Muscovado sugar

½ teaspoon Maldon sea salt

100ml double cream

200g brambles/ blackberries

100g dark chocolate, chopped into small pieces

Serves 6-8

150g 75% plain dark chocolate

85g salted butter

100g ground almonds

3 large eggs

85g golden caster sugar

Large pinch of cream of tartar

Icing sugar or cocoa to dust (optional)

FUDGY CHOCOLATE CAKE

Linda Tubby

This flourless chocolate cake uses whisked egg whites to create a meringue and provide volume and to give a light texture. You will need a 20cm springform tin greased and fully lined with baking parchment.

———

Preheat the oven to 180ºC/160ºC fan/Gas 4.

Break the chocolate into a medium-sized bowl. Cut the butter into chunks and add to the bowl. Sit the bowl over a small pan of just-simmering water, making sure the base of the bowl does not touch the water. Melt the chocolate and butter together for about 5 minutes. Remove from the heat and stir to melt completely. Mix in the almonds and set aside.

Separate the eggs into two large bowls and add half the sugar to the yolks. Add the cream of tartar to the whites and whisk until soft peaks form. Gradually add the rest of the sugar, whisking between each addition to create a stiff meringue.

Without washing the beaters whisk the yolks and sugar together until creamy and the whisk leaves a trail. Fold in the chocolate almond mixture and mix well to combine. Gently fold in the meringue and keep folding until the mixture is even in colour.

Spoon the mixture into the prepared springform tin and bake for 25–30 minutes until risen. It will still be quite soft in the middle but it firms up as it cools. When cold, if wished, dust with icing sugar or cocoa to serve.

THE PASSAGE
to ending homelessness

Cliff
Volunteer

CHOCOLATE TIRAMISU

Rory Bremner

My daughter needed to cook an Italian meal – Tiramisu seemed the perfect pudding. But my wife doesn't like coffee! So I adapted a recipe in a book given to me by Antonio Carluccio and used drinking chocolate instead of coffee!

_____

Make a small (half) cup of drinking chocolate and allow it to cool. Then soak the sponge biscuits briefly in the drinking chocolate to soften but not break up.

Mix the egg yolk, caster sugar, vanilla essence and sherry with the mascarpone in a bowl and stir all into a cream. Add a dash of the drinking chocolate to the mixture.

Form a layer with half the sponge biscuits in an oblong glass bowl. Cover with half the mascarpone mix, then add another layer of biscuits, before covering with the rest of the mascarpone mixture. Grate chocolate over the top and place in fridge for an hour or two before serving.

Serves 4

Drinking chocolate

Box of Italian sponge biscuits (Savoyard biscuits)

1 large egg yolk

50g caster sugar

Vanilla essence

1 v small glass of sherry (or kahlua, or amaretto, whatever's to hand)

300ml mascarpone

50g dark chocolate for grating

Cliff Black - volunteer

Cliff started working aged about 16 years in sales jobs and other odd jobs, he then worked in the fashion world - as a sales assistant for Next, and for a Spanish clothing outlet as well as some others for several years but he never found the perfect employment or was able to settle. He last worked as a police officer until 1999 when he got sick and had to leave; they were a really good employer. He had to isolate himself to get stronger. In April 2017 he went to an Open Day for Volunteers in East London where two people from The Passage had a stall. Now he works for them three days a week in the kitchen. He says the routine does him good and every shift is different. Giving time to the clients should be genuine and lovely, and often they share their details with him. In 2019 Cliff won Charity Job's Star Homelessness Volunteer 2019 award, which he says was totally unexpected.

Cliff, now 51 years old, is a generous hearted volunteer, friends with lots of the clients. He has many interests - is currently on level two of a gym certification course, plays classical and jazz clarinet, the piano and he speaks Spanish, Italian, French and Greek. He was born of Jamaican parents in East London, one of seven kids. Positive thinking is his goal.

Serves 12

100g butter

2 tablespoons
caster sugar

150g strong
white flour

4 eggs

For the chocolate covering:

200g Chocolate Orange

750ml double cream

2 tablespoons
caster sugar

1 vanilla pod

CHOCOLATE ORANGE PROFITEROLES

Micky Bottone

I decided to use this recipe as it was one of the dishes I learnt, as a trainee chef, at the Army and Navy Club in Pall Mall.

———

Preheat the oven to 200ºC/180ºC fan/Gas 6.

Put the butter into a pan with 300ml cold water. Heat gently until the butter has melted, then add the caster sugar; when the sugar has melted, remove the pan from the heat.

Stir in the flour and work the mixture until the paste comes away from the sides of the pan and looks smooth and lump-free. This requires some vigorous mixing!

When the dough has cooled, add the eggs, one at a time, beating energetically until the mixture is smooth, glossy and pliant.

Spoon the paste into a piping bag. Lightly flour a baking tray and pipe small twists of the mixture onto the tray. Make sure, as you fill the tray with twists, to allow space for the choux pastry to rise and spread as it cooks. Put into the preheated oven for 20 minutes, when they should have risen. Remove from the oven and place on a wire rack. Insert a knife into the bottom of each profiterole and make a small opening. Allow to cool to room temperature.

Meanwhile, make the chocolate covering – break up the Chocolate Orange into a bowl and place the bowl over a pan of simmering water and allow to melt gently. When stirred it should be smooth and glossy.

Whip the cream with the sugar and the seeds from the vanilla pod until the peaks of cream stay up on their own. Place in the fridge.

When ready to serve, fill a piping bag with the cream mix. Pick up a profiterole and gently insert and squeeze the contents into the opening you made earlier. Then dip the profiterole into the chocolate sauce and place on a serving tray. Repeat until all are filled and covered.

GROWN-UP BREAD & BUTTER PUDDING

Jo Fairley

———

Preheat the oven to 150ºC/130ºC fan/Gas 2.

Remove crusts and butter two-thirds of the loaf. Cut the slices into triangles and arrange one layer in a dish (preferably a square ceramic/Le Creuset dish).

Grate 50g of chocolate and set aside.

Melt the rest of the chocolate in a large bowl set over a pan of simmering water and slowly add the milk, stirring all the time. Turn off the heat but leave in the saucepan, adding the vanilla. Beat the eggs and add to the chocolate mixture. Pour the mixture over the first layer of bread and butter, sprinkle with sugar (to taste), and continue to layer the bread and butter and chocolate sauce until it's all used up, finishing the top with buttered triangles (butter up). Sprinkle with sugar, extra knobs of butter and the grated chocolate.

Place in the oven and add more butter knobs. If the top darkens too fast, remove and cover in foil, cooking for around an hour in all.

Serve with Green & Black's Vanilla Ice Cream or thick double cream.

Lie down afterwards.

Serves 6–8

1 sliced organic white loaf

Organic butter

3 x 100g bars Green & Black's Dark Chocolate

250ml milk

6 drops vanilla essence

4 large organic eggs

Organic caster sugar

HEDGEHOG IN THE SNOW

Tom Holland

A poem by Philip Larkin which most haunts me describes how, mowing the lawn, he accidentally ran over a hedgehog. He had not meant to kill the animal – he just hadn't seen it. Mourning the creature's death, he was prompted to this reflection:

> '… we should be careful
> Of each other, we should be kind
> While there is still time.'

This, now that hedgehog numbers in Britain are plummeting, seems an admirable reflection. Nobody wants hedgehogs to go extinct but we are killing them all the same. The message, though, has an applicability far beyond the dimension of wildlife conservation. We kill people as well as hedgehogs by closing our eyes to them. This is why – 'While there is still time' – we should always aim to be kind.

———

Preheat the oven to 180ºC/160ºC fan/Gas 4. Butter a 20cm springform cake tin and line the base with baking parchment.

Using electric beaters, cream the sugar with egg yolks until lighter in texture and colour, about 5 minutes. Add the chestnut purée, cinnamon, vanilla and almonds. Melt the chocolate in a bowl over a pan of simmering water. Fold into the mixture.

Whisk the egg whites until peaks form. Fold gently into the mixture, using a metal spoon. Pour into the tin and bake for 35 minutes. Remove and let cool in the tin.

Turn out the cake and place it on a serving plate. Decide where the hedgehog's nose is going to be, and cut a slice from this point to halfway up the cake. Repeat on the other side. Lay these spare slices, side by side and flat side down, on the top of the rest of the cake, to create the rough shape of the hedgehog's body.

Make the snowy frosting by putting all the ingredients in a large bowl over a pan of simmering water. Place over a medium heat on the hob. Whisk (electric easier) until the mixture forms stiff peaks. Using a spatula, drop the mixture evenly onto the cake, ensuring the entire surface is covered, allowing a bit extra for a snout. Use the point of a knife to draw up the mixture to create little peaks around the whole body of the hedgehog, leaving a space for the creature's eyes and snout. Make its eyes with blueberries, nose with a blackberry, and spines with almonds. Serve at room temperature.

On the street

Sat in the centre of Victoria, lonely, feeling unloved, having no one, is the worst disease that any human being can ever experience.

Serves 4

A little butter for greasing

220g caster sugar

4 eggs, separated

200g sachet unsweetened chestnut purée

1 teaspoon ground cinnamon

1 teaspoon vanilla essence

50g ground almonds

150g dark chocolate

For the snowy frosting:
340g caster sugar

4 tablespoons water

½ teaspoon cream of tartar

2 egg whites, unwhipped

½ teaspoon salt

1 teaspoon vanilla essence

Final touches:
2 blueberries

1 blackberry

50g sliced blanched almonds

DELIZIA AL LIMONE

Massimo Cartino

Serves 9

5 eggs, separated

90g sugar

Finely grated zest of 1 lemon

½ vanilla pod

40g plain white flour

25g cornflour

Pinch of salt

For the lemon cream:
Finely grated zest and juice of 1 lemon

2 egg yolks

40g sugar

40g butter

For the lemon pastry cream:
150ml milk

80ml cream

Finely grated zest of 1 lemon

4 egg yolks

60g sugar

½ vanilla pod

15g cornflour

Pinch of salt

For the limoncello syrup:
30g sugar

30ml water

Finely grated zest of half a lemon

30ml limoncello

To assemble:
125ml whipped cream

Candied lemon peel

I was working in the hotel industry at a restaurant; I had a job and a place to live connected to my work. I started having alcohol problems and it all got too much, I was feeling worse and worse, and then one day it got very bad. I lost my job, so I lost my home. I came to The Passage and they helped me to slowly recover. At the end of May 2020, Michael at Passage House helped me move into my own place.

———

Preheat the oven to 170ºC/150ºC fan/Gas 3. Grease three hemisphere moulds or tins approximately 6–8cm in diameter or use a silicone hemisphere mould tray.

Make the sponge cake by beating the egg yolks with the sugar, lemon zest and the seeds scraped from the vanilla pod in a bowl.

In a separate bowl, beat the egg whites into stiff peaks, then gently incorporate them into the egg mixture. Add the flour, cornflour and salt to the mixture. Pour into the prepared tins or moulds and cook for about 15 minutes. Remove the cakes from the oven, leave in the tins for 15–20 minutes then turn out onto a cooling rack and leave to cool for 1½ hours.

Then make the lemon cream: leave the lemon zest to soak in the juice for about 20 minutes. Beat the yolks with the sugar and add the lemon juice and zest. Pour the mixture into a saucepan and cook over a low heat until it reaches 80ºC and forms a cream. Remove the pan from the heat and leave it cool to about 50ºC then add the butter in pieces until it melts completely. Refrigerate.

Next make the lemon pastry cream: put the milk, cream and lemon zest in a saucepan over a medium heat, bring to the boil then turn off and leave to infuse for about 1 hour.

Beat the yolks with the sugar, seeds scraped from the vanilla pod, cornflour and salt, then slowly add the milk and cream mixture. Return it to the saucepan over gentle heat. Stir until the cream thickens, then remove from the heat and allow to cool fully then store in the fridge.

Finally tackle the limoncello syrup: mix the sugar with the water and lemon zest in a pan over a low heat for 1 minute. Leave to cool then stir in the limoncello.

To assemble the cakes, mix the lemon cream and lemon pastry cream together and add to a piping bag. Make a little hole in the base of each sponge cake with a sharp knife. Fill the sponge cakes with cream through the holes, right to the top.

Add the remaining lemon cream to the whipped cream to make a thick glaze. Using a toothpick, prick the sponges all over. Brush the cakes with the limoncello syrup then cover them with the glaze and refrigerate for a couple of hours. Just before serving, decorate the cakes with the candied lemon peel.

LEFTOVER PANETTONE BREAD & NUTELLA PUDDING

Julie Etchingham

If you live in any of our big cities, you can't fail to have noticed the ever-growing scandal of the number of people living on our streets, without a place to call home. If I'm walking up from Waterloo to our newsroom, in the busyness of a working day, I can lose track of how many are there. Pope Francis encourages us not just to give to the homeless, but to truly recognise them and look them in the eye – to connect, in full human solidarity and compassion. Not many of us can say we live up to this.

But it's the driving force and vision of the wonderful team at The Passage – helping 200 men and women every day. Sometimes they catch people just before they fall into street homelessness. Often, they are there to give shelter and support to those whose lives are lost in this trauma of not having a place to call home. They give their time, energy, expertise and compassion where many of us can't, don't or won't. When the world turns its face away, too distracted, too busy – The Passage never does.

Thank you so much for buying this book in solidarity with their life-giving work. I am a terrible cook, but this one just about lashes up OK after Christmas when no one is casting too critical an eye. It is even better cold the next morning, straight out the fridge when no one is looking…

———

Preheat the oven to 160ºC/140ºC fan/Gas 3.

Liberally spread the panettone with Nutella and lay the slices neatly or messily in a 20 x 30cm ovenproof dish.

Whisk together the whole eggs, egg yolk, milk, cream, Bailey's and caster sugar in a large mixing bowl. Pour some of the egg mixture over the slices of panettone and allow to rest for 5 minutes. Repeat the process a couple of times, until all the creamy, boozy mixture is used up.

Sprinkle some Demerara sugar on top and bake for 25–30 minutes until golden brown but still a bit wobbly. Serve with cream to delighted guests.

Serves 4–6

250g panettone, cut into 1cm slices

Couple of tablespoons of Nutella

2 free-range eggs, plus 1 egg yolk

200ml full-fat milk

200ml double cream

Dash of Bailey's Irish Cream

60g caster sugar

Demerara sugar for dusting

Pouring cream to serve

BROWN BUTTER, APPLE & FIG FLAPJACK

John Whaite

Flapjack is a perfect example of balance: a sweet treat that conveys a decent amount of nourishment. While the sugar and butter clearly signal that this is a treat to be enjoyed only occasionally, there is still much virtue to be found in the humble classic. Oats are packed with magnesium – a mineral that is vital for regulating blood pressure and helping to reduce the risk of heart attack and stroke. And, there's also wide data to suggest a lack of magnesium correlates closely with depression. It's plain to see that oats should be a vital part of your diet.

Dried apple, while added primarily for flavour, also offers dietary fibre – as do the oats – which helps to regulate the body's absorption of carbohydrates and so reduce spikes in blood sugar. It's full of key B vitamins, too. Dried figs contribute to dietary fibre as well, but they're also a great source of calcium and potassium, important minerals for maintaining strong bones and for reducing the risk of osteoporosis. It seems there's far more to the humble flapjack than its heavenly chewiness.

————

Preheat the oven to 180ºC/160ºC fan/Gas 4 and grease and line a 20 x 30cm baking tin with baking parchment.

First make the brown butter. Put the cubed butter into a medium-sized saucepan and set over a high heat. Once melted, the butter will start to bubble violently, this is just the excess moisture evaporating. Swirl the pan every 30 seconds or so as the butter spits at you. When the bubbling subsides, and a fine cappuccino-like foam appears on the surface accompanied by a rich nutty smell, remove the pan from the heat and add the sugar and honey. Stir to dissolve the sugar.

In a mixing bowl toss together the oats, dried fruit and crushed Ryvita, then add the butter mixture. Stir to combine everything really well – the oats should be completely damp from the brown butter. Tip the mixture into the prepared baking tin and press down to level and compact the oaty rubble as tightly as possible. Bake for 20 minutes, press down again – though carefully, as it will be very hot – then bake for a further 10–15 minutes, until lightly browned. Cool completely in the tin, then tip onto a chopping board and cut into 16 triangles.

Makes 16

250g salted butter, cubed

120g light brown muscovado sugar

180g runny honey

375g jumbo oats

100g dried apple pieces, chopped

100g dried figs, chopped

45g dark Ryvita crackers, crushed

EASY STICKY TOFFEE PUDDING

Nigella Lawson

This is just what you want for a Sunday lunch, cosy and comforting and indulgent. You might need a brisk walk afterwards!

———

Preheat the oven to 190ºC/170ºC fan/Gas 5 and butter a 1.5-litre capacity pudding dish.

Combine the 100g of dark muscovado sugar with the flour in a large bowl. Pour the milk into a measuring jug, beat in the egg, vanilla and melted butter and then pour this mixture over the sugar and flour, stirring – just with a wooden spoon – to combine. Fold in the dates then scrape into the prepared pudding dish. Don't worry if it doesn't look very full: it will do by the time it cooks.

Sprinkle over the 200g of dark muscovado sugar and dot with the butter. Pour over the boiling water (yes really!) and transfer to the oven. Set the timer for 45 minutes, though you might find the pudding needs 5 or 10 minutes more. The top of the pudding should be springy and spongy when it's cooked; underneath, the butter, dark muscovado sugar and boiling water will have turned into a rich, sticky sauce. Serve with vanilla ice cream, crème fraîche, double or single cream as you wish.

Serves 6–8

100g dark muscovado sugar

175g self-raising flour

125ml full-fat milk

1 large egg

1 teaspoon vanilla extract

50g unsalted butter, melted

200g dates, chopped

For the sauce:
200g dark muscovado sugar

Approx. 25g unsalted butter, in little blobs

500ml boiling water

Serves 8–10

270g whole almonds blanched and peeled (do not be lured towards the awful bought ground matter)

120g plain flour

270g unsalted butter

5 well-sized best eggs

320g caster sugar

1 vanilla pod

Finely grated zest of 1 orange

Juice of 2 oranges

1 tablespoon icing sugar

Handful of flaked almonds, baked until golden

For the curd:
15 clementines

2 best eggs

100g caster sugar

110g unsalted butter

ALMOND CAKE, CLEMENTINE CURD & NAUGHTY JERSEY CREAM

Jeremy Lee

Cakes made with best-quality eggs and butter, sweetened with sugar give a real boost of energy. When paired with a curd rich in vitamins from citrus fruits, here clementines, this pudding delivers very wonderful sense of comfort and joy. We find that grinding almonds gives a much more pleasing quality to the cake, not to mention flavour and feel strongly too that the properties of the almond are best expressed. We have cooked this cake for many, many years and have grown to love it so much that we feel always that it is a recipe that wins cooked thusly. We hope that you enjoy this cake as much as we do at Quo Vadis, and at the very least that it nourishes the soul.

———

Preheat the oven to 180ºC/160ºC fan/Gas 4. Line a 24/25cm cake tin with baking parchment.

Ensure the almonds are dry, then grind them until fine and add to the flour.

Meanwhile place the butter in a pan and melt over a gentle heat.

Crack the eggs into a bowl, add the sugar and beat well until pale. Split the vanilla pod lengthwise and scrape out the seeds, then add to the bowl and beat, before adding in the orange zest. Deftly add the almonds and flour and, with great care, slowly add the melted butter.

Pour the batter into the lined cake tin and bake in the oven for 45–50 minutes until risen and golden. The time-honoured insertion of skewer to ensure doneness is appropriate.

Whisk together the orange juice and icing sugar while the cake is still warm and spoon over to give the lightest glaze.

To make the curd, carefully zest the clementines then halve and squeeze to extract the juice. Sieve the juice into a heavy-bottomed saucepan, then add in the zest, eggs, sugar and butter. Place the pan over a low heat and stir gently until the curd thickens, about 10 minutes or so. Tip the curd into a bowl, cool, cover and refrigerate.

To serve, slice the warm cake, pour on a spoonful of curd, then add a spoonful of the very best Jersey cream. Strew with the flaked almonds and take a bow.

Serves 6-8

115g pistachios,
finely ground
(or, for ease,
use ground almonds)

225g plain spelt flour

2 teaspoons
baking powder

260g unsalted butter,
really soft

4 large eggs

130g honey (or golden
caster sugar)

130g coconut sugar

Finely grated zest
of 2 limes

For the cream:
350ml double cream

2 heaped tablespoons
natural Greek
yogurt

2 teaspoons sugar

1 teaspoon rose water,
or to taste (if using
rose essence, it's much
stronger so be careful
not to add too much)

To decorate:
6 tablespoons plum or
strawberry jam

300g strawberries,
hulled and cut in
half lengthways

Unrefined icing sugar
for dusting

FRAGRANT STRAWBERRIES WITH LAYERS OF PISTACHIO SPONGE & ROSE CREAM

Amber Rose

I made this cake around the time my little girl was turning 1 year old for her birthday. She was born when all the roses in our neighbourhood were in full bloom and strawberries are also at their best, so naturally I put these ingredients together to create a lovely festive seasonal cake for her. It's a rather decadent take on the classic Victoria sponge, with a little extra layer and a few more flavours, just for celebratory joy. You could also use ground almonds if that's easier. The ground nuts do create a lovely moist sponge and standing the little strawberries upright gives them a beautifully interesting look as the icing sugar will stay dusted on the uncut side but will melt on the cut side – so you get gorgeous jewel-like reds and contrasting whites.

———————

Preheat the oven to 180ºC/160ºC fan/Gas 4 and line three 20cm loose-based sandwich tins.

Grind the pistachios by placing them in a mini chopper, food processor or high-powered blender and blitz to quite a fine meal. (Don't go too far as it's possible to turn your nuts into nut butter if you blend for too long.)

Sift the flour and bakig powder into the bowl of a free-standing mixer, then add all the other cake ingredients. Mix slowly at first, using the whisk attachment, then gradually turn up the speed as the mix starts to come together. Don't over-mix: you want a light cake. After a minute or two, no more, when the batter looks thoroughly combined, scrape into your prepared tins and bake for 25–30 minutes, or until golden and risen, and the centre springs back after a gentle press. Or insert a skewer or thin sharp knife into the middle – if it comes out clean then the cakes are cooked.

Remove the cakes from the oven and leave to cool in the tins for 5 minutes before carefully turning out onto a cooling rack. When the cakes are cold you can get on with making the rose cream.

Lightly whip the cream, yogurt, sugar and rose water until soft peaks form, being very careful not to overmix or the cream will start to curdle.

To decorate, place one cake on a serving platter, evenly spread 2 tablespoons of jam over the surface, then spoon a third of the whipped rose cream on top. Top with the second cake and repeat the layers of jam and cream.

Place the third cake on top, once again repeating the layers of jam and cream. Then carefully poke the long strawberry halves into the cream layer so that they are standing with their pointy sides uppermost. When all the berries are placed you can give the entire cake a light dusting with unrefined icing sugar as a final flourish. Serve right away with a cup of wonderfully fragrant herbal tea, such as fresh pineapple sage, lemon balm or lemon verbena, or mint.

Mitchel Ceney - client

Mitchel comes from Dudley in the West Midlands. He has two kids with whom he keeps up, but no relationship with his parents and immediate family. After years of being street homeless, problems with drug addiction and spells in prison, in June 2019 he was referred by the Outreach services in Victoria to Passage House Assessment Centre. He's successfully completed the 'Ready to Rent' course and is participating with great enthusiasm in the Art Group with David Tovey, a formerly homeless artist who has exhibited widely, including at the Tate Modern, and is founder of One Festival of Homeless Art. Mitchel wants to work in the field of art or music. He does beautiful drawings and calligraphy, including the artwork for the 'Secret Santa Box' at Passage House. He says that with money, his will power to keep off drugs weakens and that he misses his ex-girlfriend who has moved back to Poland. But he is determined to build a life for himself now.

Serves 10-12

250g butter

250g caster sugar

3 large eggs, beaten

150g polenta bramata

250g ground almonds

Finely grated zest
and juice of
2 large oranges

For the topping:
250g honey

Juice of 1 lemon

Juice of 1 orange
(use 1 of the
oranges above)

To serve:
50g whole pistachio
nuts, shelled

Approx. 4 tablespoons
honey

150ml natural Greek
yogurt

GREEK ORANGE CAKE WITH HONEY & PISTACHIOS

Charlotte Pike

This special cake is packed with vibrant flavours, making it both delicious and satisfying. It is equally good served as a sweet treat with a cup of tea or coffee, or as a memorable pudding.

The bright citrus and honey flavours are inspired by Greece, and the fragrant topping and sprinkling of crunchy nuts are reminiscent of the delicious sticky cakes found in bakeries right across the Greek mainland and islands.

Naturally gluten-free, this is a good cake to make for anyone avoiding wheat, and its nut-heavy base makes it sustaining and nourishing.

If you make the cake in advance, leave the nuts off and sprinkle them on the top just before serving, to retain their crispness.

———

Preheat oven to 180ºC/160ºC fan/Gas 4. Grease and line a 24cm springform tin with baking parchment.

In a large mixing bowl, cream together the butter and sugar. Add the eggs and beat to incorporate, followed by the polenta and ground almonds, and mix well; finally add the orange zest and the juice of 1 orange. Keep the juice of the second orange for the topping.

Transfer the mixture to the tin, level off and bake for 30–40 minutes until it's an even golden brown.

Meanwhile, warm the honey, remaining orange and lemon juice in a small pan over a moderate heat. Stir gently until the honey and citrus juices blend together.

When the cake is baked, remove from the oven, prick well with a cocktail stick and then pour over the syrup-like topping. Set the cake aside to cool. Before you turn the oven off, tip the pistachios onto a little tray and roast for around 7 minutes. Remove from the oven and set aside to cool.

Once the cake is cool, chop the pistachios and sprinkle over the cake. Stir the honey into the Greek yogurt and serve on the side, to spoon onto the cake.

PEAR, APPLE & RASPBERRY CRUMBLE WITH ORANGE BLOSSOM CREAM

Ghillie James

As we sit down to eat as a family, I am always reminded how extremely lucky I am to have a kitchen table that is surrounded by chatter and laughter as we share precious time together. There are many who don't have a kitchen table. Nor do they have comforting food, or the support and love of a family. I hate that thought. I spent two Christmases in the 90s volunteering for Crisis at Christmas. Everyone should do it. It changed the way I saw 'the homeless'. They are not just a group or a number but individuals from many walks of life who have had a really bad deal and deserve to be treated with dignity and love.

———

Preheat the oven to 180ºC/160ºC fan/Gas 4.

Put the apples and pears into a saucepan. Add the lemon juice and sugar and stir. Cook over a medium heat, stirring every so often, until the sugar has melted and the fruits are just starting to soften – about 5–8 minutes. Then add the raspberries. Transfer to a 1-litre ovenproof dish, about 6–8cm deep.

Combine the dry ingredients for the crumble. Use the blunt edge of a knife to stir in the butter in a slow trickle until it has been absorbed and the mixture resembles rubble. Scatter evenly over the fruits to entirely cover. Bake in the middle of the oven for 25–35 minutes until the crumble is golden and the juices bubble through. Mix the mascarpone with enough honey to lightly sweeten. Serve with the crumble.

Mark Batham - client

Mark has two slipped discs, a slightly twisted spine and suffers from sciatica; he is walking with a stick, waiting for an operation to cure his back problems. Brought up in London, he worked for recording studios and in the music business and became head chef at Heaven Nightclub in Charing Cross. He lived with his partner, becoming homeless after she died and the relatives pushed him out. He'd been quite spoilt and suddenly all was gone. He went wandering for six or seven years before being helped into temporary accommodation in London. His mobile was ruined when someone dropped liquid onto it and missed renewing his tenancy, being forced out. Since then he's been sofa-surfing, going over to Lisson Grove and Ladbroke Grove in Notting Hill to see his new partner; both are homeless.

Serves 4-6

850g (unpeeled weight) eating apples and pears (about 2 apples and 2 large pears, peeled, cored and cut into raspberry-sized chunks

3 tablespoons lemon juice (about half a lemon)

75g sugar

150g fresh raspberries (or you can use frozen ones, defrosted)

For the crumble topping:
125g plain or spelt flour

75g rolled oats

2 heaped tablespoons flaked almonds

85g sugar

½ teaspoon ground ginger

85g butter, melted

For the honey cream (optional):
4 heaped tablespoons mascarpone

1-2 teaspoons floral runny honey, such as orange blossom

Serve 8

20 apricots, halved and stoned

250ml dry white wine

2 teaspoons vanilla extract

85g caster sugar

For the ice cream:
6 large egg yolks

120g caster sugar

150ml full-fat milk

450ml double cream

100ml sweet Marsala

Squeeze of lemon (add it to taste)

BAKED APRICOTS WITH MARSALA ICE CREAM

Diana Henry

Baked apricots are one of the best summer desserts, at the same time tart and honeyed. They're good with a dollop of crème fraîche but are even better with Marsala ice cream (which is basically Italian zabaglione in ice-cream form). This ice is rich and silky.

———

Beat the egg yolks and sugar with an electric mixer for 2 minutes until pale and frothy. Heat the milk and cream together in a saucepan until steaming then whisk this into the egg mixture, pouring slowly and whisking all the time.

Rinse out the pan, put the egg and cream mixture into it and set it over a low heat. Cook gently, stirring all the time, until the mixture coats the back of a spoon (if you run your forefinger through the custard it should leave a channel). Don't get the mixture too hot or it will scramble.

Pour the custard into a bowl set in a sink full of cold water so that it cools quickly. Stir it every so often as it's cooling. Add the Marsala, taste and add a little lemon juice (oddly it intensifies the flavour of the Marsala but you need to be careful not to overdo it). Cover and chill the mixture in the fridge. Churn the custard in an ice-cream machine then transfer to the freezer to firm up. If you don't have an ice-cream machine put the custard into a metal container and put in the freezer. You need to remove the mixture and beat it in a food processor (in order to incorporate air into it) 3 or 4 times during the freezing process.

Preheat the oven to 190°C/170°C fan/Gas 4. Lay the apricots, skin side up, in slightly overlapping circles or rows in a shallow ovenproof dish. Mix the wine with the vanilla and pour it over. Sprinkle on the sugar. Bake for 20–25 minutes (how long it takes depends on the ripeness of the fruit) until tender and slightly caramelised in patches. Leave to cool completely.

Serve the apricots with the Marsala ice cream.

APRICOT & PISTACHIO GALETTE

Annie Rigg

———

Preheat the oven to 200ºC/180ºC fan/Gas 6 and put a solid, flat baking sheet on the middle shelf to heat up as the oven does.

Make the frangipane first: tip 50g of the pistachios into a food processor and finely chop, add the ground almonds, butter, the 75g of sugar, the whole egg, yolk, vanilla, lemon zest and a pinch of salt and mix again until smooth.

Lightly dust the work surface with flour and roll the pastry into a rough round shape – no more than 2mm thick and 30–32cm in diameter. Trim the edges to neaten the circle.

Carefully slide the pastry onto another large baking sheet that has been lined with a sheet of baking parchment. Spread the frangipane filling over the pastry, leaving a 2cm border all the way round. Arrange the apricot quarters over the frangipane and scatter with the remaining pistachios, roughly chopped. Fold the pastry edges over, pleating them as you go. Using a fork, lightly beat the egg white until foamy and brush onto the pastry border. Scatter with the remaining caster sugar and slide the galette, with the baking parchment, onto the hot tray in the preheated oven and immediately reduce the oven temperature to 180ºC/160ºC fan/Gas 4. Bake for about 30 minutes until the frangipane is golden, the pastry crisp and the apricots are tender.

Serves 6

75g pistachios

25g ground almonds

50g unsalted butter, softened

75g caster sugar, plus 1 tablespoon

2 medium eggs, 1 whole and 1 separated

1 teaspoon vanilla extract

1 teaspoon finely grated lemon zest

Pinch of salt

Plain flour for rolling out

375g all-butter puff pastry

500g apricots, quartered and stoned

Khai Halls ~ client liaison

During the coronavirus pandemic, homeless clients were moved off the streets and placed into safe temporary accommodation, such as empty hotel rooms. Khai and her team are now working to place these clients into private rented accommodation, thus preventing a return to the streets. They continue to give support to the clients once they are in their new accommodation around tenancy or benefit issues.

Each client can be referred to The Passage's Home for Good scheme where they will be matched with a volunteer, trained by The Passage, in their local area. This partnership provides the client with support and a friendly contact in their new community to help them put down roots and establish a local connection.

Serves 4

250g (roughly 5 sticks) rhubarb

400ml coconut milk

3 tablespoons agar agar

100ml maple syrup

1 tablespoon rose water

½ teaspoon ground cardamom

Fresh or dried rose petals to decorate (optional)

RHUBARB & ROSE PANNA COTTA

Rachel de Thample

This gorgeous coconut-based panna cotta with agar agar, a seaweed-based setting agent, is wonderfully luxurious. It's sweetened only with maple syrup and is rich in protein and seasonal fruit, making it a nourishing spring dessert.

———

Preheat your oven to 180ºC/160ºC fan/Gas 4.

Cut the rhubarb into 4cm batons and arrange half of them on a roasting tray. Slide into the oven to bake for 10–15 minutes or until just softened but not broken down.

Blend the remaining rhubarb with the coconut milk and agar agar until the rhubarb is fully whipped into the coconut milk. Pour into a saucepan and simmer for 5 minutes. Then press through a fine mesh sieve to strain out the strands of rhubarb and any undissolved bits of agar.

Whisk in the maple syrup, rose water and cardamom. Pour into ramekins. Tuck pieces of roasted rhubarb into each one.

Put in the fridge to set for at least 4 hours – or you can cheat and freeze for 30 minutes to 1 hour – just make sure it sets and doesn't freeze. Decorate with rose petals, if you have them.

THE PASSAGE
to ending homelessness

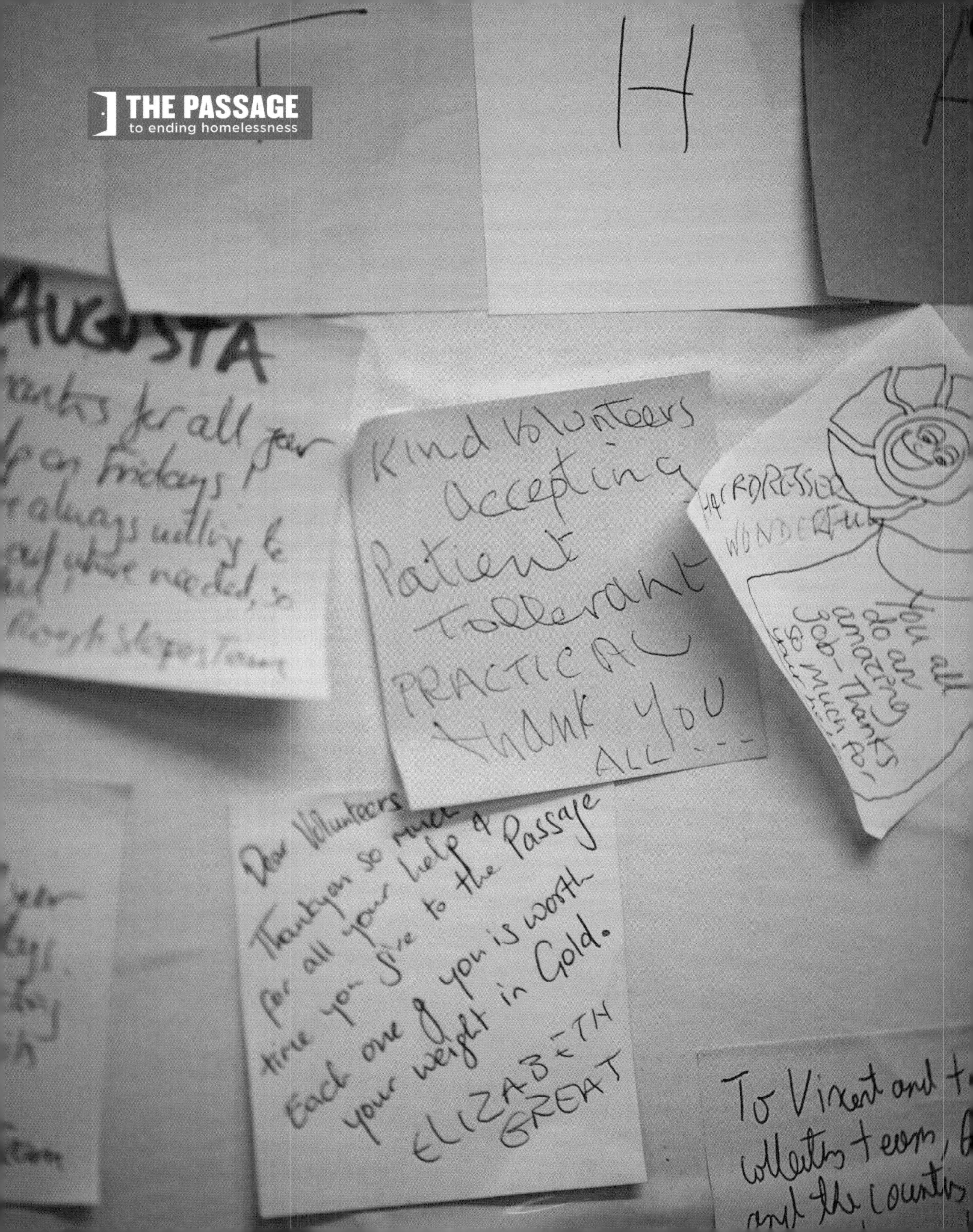

RHUBARB & CUSTARD MILLEFEUILLE

Oliver Gladwin

In life, there are few childhood foody memories as good as rhubarb and custard in the British countryside, where my mother taught us three brothers the value of good seasonal food. I have recreated that taste sensation but with some cheffy techniques and a beautiful light crispy dessert. You will need a good blitzer.

———

Generously dust the pastry with icing sugar and roll it out to the size of a baking sheet. Lay the pastry on the baking sheet and cut into rectangles (roughly 18–24 pieces), then lay another baking sheet of the same size on top. The second sheet will stop the pasty rising and the icing sugar will create a caramel effect. Bake at 180ºC/160ºC fan/Gas 4 for 20 minutes.

To make the custard-set cream, warm the cream, sugar and vanilla pod in a pan to dissolve the sugar and infuse the vanilla. Bring to the boil, whisk in the agar agar, then boil for 2 minutes. Whisk the egg yolks into the milk, then add the mixture to the cream mixture, and continue whisking until it begins to set. Pour into a tub and set in the fridge. Blitz the set cream until smooth and store in a piping bag.

To make the rhubarb, mix the ingredients and lay in a shallow casserole topped with baking parchment. Bake for just 10 minutes at 150ºC/130ºC fan/Gas 2, stirring a couple of times, then allow to cool in its juices before transferring to a 2-litre tub.

To make the purée, cook the rhubarb and sugar with a little water until the sugar melts and the liquid boils. Add in the citric acid and the agar agar, boil for 2 minutes, then blitz. Test for seasoning and add more sugar if too tart. Allow to cool and then blitz again until smooth.

To make the candied crisp, make a light sugar syrup melting the sugar in 100ml water over gentle heat and then slicing the rhubarb very thinly lengthways, about 7.5–10cm long and using tweezers or tongs, submerge the rhubarb in the syrup one by one, and then lay them out on baking parchment. Place in a very low oven (110ºC/90ºC fan/Gas ¼) for 20 minutes. Allow to cool. For the baked white chocolate, put the chocolate on a baking tray. Bake at 110ºC/90ºC fan/Gas ¼ for 20 minutes. Remove and set aside until cold and then crumble.

To assemble the plate, form a layer of custard-set cream by piping in rows, then lay a rectangle of pastry over it, continue with a layer of custard-set cream, then pastry, diced rhubarb, then pastry. Top with custard-set cream, rhubarb purée, and the baked white chocolate. Then decorate with flowers of your choice.

Thank you - goes a long way.

Serves 6-8

1 packet ready-rolled puff pastry

100g icing sugar

For the custard-set cream:
300ml double cream

60g sugar

1 small vanilla pod

5g agar agar

300ml milk

4 large egg yolks

For the rhubarb:
300g diced rhubarb

70g caster sugar

30ml beetroot juice

For the purée:
330g rhubarb

100g sugar

5g citric acid

3g agar agar

For the candied crisp:
50g sugar

70g rhubarb

For the baked chocolate:
30g white chocolate

Generous handful of edible flowers - rose petals, marigolds, violas to decorate

Serves 4

250g raspberries

150ml double or whipping cream

2 teaspoons icing sugar

100g meringue nests

100g white chocolate, roughly chopped

4 sprigs of fresh mint (optional)

RASPBERRY ETON MESS

Jon Snow

Before I became a journalist, I worked with a homeless project for three years. That was over 40 years ago – things were bad then – they are far worse today. The need is great, only matched by the degree of suffering that homelessness brings for the individual. There is no more poignant moment in the year than today to remember them.

———

Mash half the raspberries with a fork; chop the rest of the fruit and put to one side.

Whip the cream with the icing sugar until soft peaks form. Gently stir the chopped fruit into the whipped cream until just combined.

Crush the meringue nests using your fingers and add the meringue pieces and white chocolate to the cream. Very gently stir through the mashed fruit to create a swirly effect.

Spoon into serving dishes, cover and refrigerate until ready to serve. Garnish with fresh mint if desired.

Here are some services that The Passage provides:

Rough Sleepers Team: immediate services including meals, showers, clothing, laundry, medical appointments, mental health and substance misuse support.

Client Development Team: advice on benefit entitlement, training, and employment opportunities, immigration legal advice, life skills development, group activities.

Housing Options Service: advice and support for single men and women who are at risk of becoming homeless.

NO-CHURN ROASTED STRAWBERRY ICE CREAM

Liz Earle

I am very thankful for not only a roof over my head, but also a garden with a veg patch for homegrown fruit and veggies. It's such a treat to be able to pick-my-own, even if I do have to race the rabbits!

————

Preheat the oven to 120ºC/100ºC/Gas 1. Put the strawberries on a large roasting tray lined with baking parchment. Drizzle with honey and a pinch of salt. Pop in the oven and roast for around 1 hour until caramelised.

Reserve a small bowl of the roasted strawberries and the syrup for serving. Blitz half the remaining strawberries in a food processor and set to one side.

In a bowl, whip up the double cream with the kefir until it starts to thicken and form stiff peaks. Beat in the condensed milk. Fold through the intact roasted strawberries.

Scoop into a freezable container and stir through the strawberry pulp to create a marbled effect. Freeze for at least 8 hours.

Serve a few scoops per person with the reserved roasted strawberries on top (they should be sticky), the syrup and a few small basil leaves on each bowl.

Serves 3 hungry people or 4 otherwise

1kg strawberries (British, ideally) washed, hulled and halved

Generous drizzle of honey

300ml double cream

200ml kefir

1 x 397g tin condensed milk

Sea salt

Basil leaves to serve

Serves 12

500g fresh mixed berries (or you can use frozen ones, defrosted)

100g caster sugar

3 medium free-range eggs

1 teaspoon vanilla extract

150g icing sugar

400g whipping or double cream

2 tablespoons cassis or cherry brandy (optional)

80-100g ready made meringues, coarsely crushed

100g dark chocolate, roughly chopped

BERRY & CHOCOLATE CHIP SEMIFREDDO

Alison Oakervee

Line a 1.5-litre loaf tin with a double layer of cling film, allowing enough overhang in each direction to fully cover the surface of the filling.

Put the berries and caster sugar in a pan with a splash of water, bring to a simmer and gently cook, uncovered, for about 20 minutes, or until they are very soft and collapsing. Place a sieve over a bowl and pour in the cooked fruit, sieve the fruit using the back of a spoon, so that all that remains are the pips. Discard the pips and allow the fruit purée to cool.

Put the eggs, vanilla extract and sugar in a bowl over a pan of simmering water. Using an electric whisk, whisk the eggs for about 5 minutes, or until the mixture has increased in volume and leaves a ribbon trail on the surface of the liquid when the beaters are lifted. Remove from the heat and continue to whisk for another 5 minutes, then leave to cool.

Meanwhile, whisk the cream until it forms stiff peaks, fold in the whipped egg mixture, along with three-quarters of the berry sauce and cassis (if using) until completely mixed together. Fold into the mixture three-quarters of the crushed meringue and all the chopped chocolate, then pour into the prepared loaf tin cover with the overhanging cling film, and freeze for 6 hours, or overnight.

Remove from the freezer about 30 minutes before serving and invert onto a serving board or plate. Serve sliced with a little of the reserved berry sauce, a few fresh berries and scatter with a little of the crushed meringue.

AMERICAN BLUEBERRY PANCAKES WITH CINNAMON YOGURT

Georgina Fuggle

In our household there are everyday pancakes, those that are cooked quickly and filled with what's left in the fridge. Then there are birthday pancakes. These have become expected, a tradition of sorts, puffed and piled high with blueberries, dripping honey and thick yogurt. More often than not, there's a birthday candle plunged into the top of the pile and an enthusiastic rendition of happy birthday accompanying them to the table.

———

Separate the eggs into two bowls – yolks in one, whites in another. Add the milk, plain flour, baking powder, sugar and salt to the yolks bowl and whisk together to form a smooth batter.

Whisk the egg whites using an electric whisk until they form soft peaks – they should be white and voluminous but not too stiff. Use a large metal spoon to fold the whites into the batter, trying to keep as much air in as possible. Transfer the mixture to a large jug.

Gently heat the oil in a large frying pan and wipe out the excess with a paper towel. Pour some batter into the pan to form small circles, roughly 6cm across. Place a few blueberries on top of each one and cook over a medium heat till bubbles appear in the centre of each pancake.

Lift the edge of the pancakes to check underneath: they should be golden brown. Then flip and cook on the other side for another 2 minutes.

To make the cinnamon yogurt, simply mix together the honey, cinnamon and yogurt and spoon on top of the pancakes.

Serve the pancakes, topped with extra blueberries and a couple of mint leaves.

Serves 4
(Makes 12 pancakes)

3 medium eggs

120ml milk

120g plain flour

1½ teaspoons baking powder

2 teaspoons caster sugar

Pinch of salt

1 teaspoon vegetable oil

Small handful of fresh blueberries, about 60g, plus extra to serve

Mint leaves to serve (optional)

For the cinnamon yogurt:
1 tablespoon runny honey

¼ teaspoon ground cinnamon

200g natural Greek-style yogurt

Serves 6

1kg mixed summer
fruits: strawberries,
hulled and quartered,
blackberries,
redcurrants,
raspberries,
loganberries,
blueberries

200g caster sugar

400g brioche loaf

SUMMER PUDDING

Claudette Dawkins

_____

Remove any stems from the berries. Wash and place them in a pan except for the strawberries. Add 3 tablespoons of water and the sugar. Gently heat for about 3 minutes until the juices from the fruit start to seep out. Add the strawberries and cook for 2 minutes more. Drain the juice from the fruit through a sieve into a bowl. Taste the juice and add more sugar if necessary.

Line a 1.5-litre pudding basin with a double layer of cling film, ensuring there is an overhang. Slice the brioche into 1cm-thick slices and remove the crusts Cut a circle of brioche big enough to fit the bottom of the basin. Line the sides of the basin with brioche, cutting to fit as necessary.

Starting with the circle, at the bottom of the bowl, dip the pieces of brioche into the fruit juice and put back into the bowl. If there are any gaps use the off-cuts to fill. Ensure you have enough brioche to cover the top.

Fill the lined basin with the fruits. Cover the fruits with a layer of brioche and pour any remaining juice over the top. Wrap the overhanging cling film over the top.

Place a small plate that will fit snugly inside the basin over the top of the pudding and use a couple of unopened 400g tins to weigh down the pudding. Place it in the fridge, weighted down, overnight.

To serve, remove the tins and the plate. Unwrap the cling film and place a serving plate over the top. Invert the pudding. Carefully remove the basin and peel away the cling film. Serve in slices.

PINEAPPLE WATER ICE

Julian Fellowes

This reminds me of my mother, who frequently made the ice on hot days in the 1950s. I wish The Passage, this marvellous charity, every possible success.

———

Dissolve the sugar in the water with the grated zest of the lemon and boil for 4 minutes. Add the lemon juice, then strain and leave to cool.

Split the pineapple in two lengthwise and slice out the flesh, discarding the tough core. Break the flesh into shreds with a fork to make around 550–600ml of pineapple pulp. Add this to the cold syrup and freeze.

If you want to, whisk the egg white until stiff and add to the ice to form a slush – about 1–2 hours after the mixture is put into the freezer.

Chill the pineapple halves for about 30 minutes in the freezer. Put the soft fruit at the bottom (reserve a few to decorate) and arrange the water ice on top. Serve immediately.

Serves 4

175g lump sugar

570ml water

Zest and juice of 1 large lemon

1 large pineapple

½ egg white (optional)

200g soft fruit (raspberries, strawberries)

Serves 4

1½ leaves gelatine

250ml double cream

75g unrefined
caster sugar

¾ vanilla pod

250ml buttermilk

3 blood oranges

BUTTERMILK & BLOOD ORANGE PANNA COTTA

Mark Flanagan

———

Soak the leaf gelatine in a bowl of ice-cold water, ensuring it is fully submerged.

Put the double cream, sugar and split vanilla pod into a saucepan and gently bring to the boil. Remove from the heat.

Once the gelatine is soft, squeeze to remove excess water. Place the gelatine into the saucepan and gently stir until completely dissolved.

Strain the cream and gelatine mix over the buttermilk and again stir gently.

Pour into a jug and keep to one side at room temperature.

Peel and segment two blood oranges, juicing the third.

Carefully place 4 blood orange segments at the bottom of four 120ml glass yogurt pots or similar vessels. Slowly pour the buttermilk panna cotta into the pots. Place in the fridge to set, ideally for 2 hours.

Sit the pots on a side plate or saucer with a teaspoon and pour some of the remaining blood orange juice over the top of the panna cotta, then serve chilled.

ORCHARD CRISP

Antony Worrall Thompson

My Orchard Crisp is good gutsy stuff with a nod to health with fruit and fibre, but to be honest when choosing a pudding, health tends to go out the window!

———

Preheat the oven to 200ºC/180ºC fan/Gas 6. Grease the bottom of a deep baking dish with extra butter.

Combine the fruit with the zest, juice, sugar, nutmeg and cordial, place in the bottom of the baking dish.

In a food processor, blend together the dry ingredients on a pulse action. Add the butter and continue to pulse until the mixture resembles coarse breadcrumbs.

Pop this mixture on top of the fruit, scatter with flaked almonds and pecans. Cover with foil and place in the oven to bake for approximately 1 hour, remove the foil and bake for a further 15 minutes or until the top is golden. Serve hot with double or clotted cream.

Home for Good

Home for Good provides ongoing support to formerly homeless people who have been resettled into their own accommodation. A person is matched with a volunteer from what might be a new local area to support them. The purpose of the service is both to help people to sustain their tenancies and to help them to settle into what will often be a new community. Through providing ongoing and holistic support at a local level we hope to reduce the number of people who return to the street after moving into accommodation.

Our Home for Good resettlement support scheme (befriending and Social Club) was nominated for a Social Integration (Innovative Project or Charity) Award at the Team London Awards 2018.

Serves 8-10

3 Bramley apples, peeled, cored and wedged

400g plums, halved and stoned

3 Conference pears, peeled, cored and cubed

Zest and juice of 1 orange and 1 lemon

4 tablespoons caster sugar

Pinch of grated nutmeg

100ml elderflower cordial

25g powdered milk

25g desiccated coconut

25g powdered almonds

25g sunflower seeds

25g rolled oats

250g plain flour

375g soft dark brown sugar

1 teaspoon ground cinnamon

½ teaspoon salt

175g unsalted butter, cut in cubes, plus extra for greasing

50g flaked almonds for scattering

50g pecans, broken for scattering

SPICED APPLES

Jeanne Strang

The spiced apple recipe is a dessert, to be served with cream or yogurt in pretty glass bowls. Any kind of dessert apples can be used, and the dried fruit would be currants and raisins. If you want to store them, put them into screwtop glass jars and they will be good for months.

———

Preheat the oven to 160ºC/140ºC fan/Gas 3.

Peel and core the apples and cut them into pieces. Put in an ovenproof pan which has a close-fitting lid. Add all the other ingredients. Heat the pan gently on the hob to melt the butter before transferring it to the oven. Cook for at least 3 hours until the fruit is soft. The longer you cook it the darker it gets.

Leave to cool a little before putting it into jam jars with screwtop lids. This makes enough to fill two jars.

Serves 4

4 dessert apples

¼ teaspoon ground cinnamon

¼ teaspoon ground nutmeg

6 cloves

60g brown sugar

1 orange, juiced, plus a piece of the peel

2 tablespoons dried fruit

30g unsalted butter

2 tablespoons calvados (or other spirit)

Zoe Minihan - Hotel School

The Hotel School is run by Zoe Minihan and, like many a good idea, came from Jeremy Goring, chief exec of The Goring Hotel, and Mick Clarke, chief exec of The Passage, sitting down for a drink! One bemoans the difficulty of getting people to work in the hospitality industry, and the other needs jobs for people recovering from problems and using The Passage's services. A Hotel School where Clients from The Passage (and other similar charities) can do a three-month course learning skills for the hospitality trade is the idea and the first course took place in April 2017. Topics taught include being a waiter, a commis chef, a kitchen porter, table-laying, baking and so forth and the Clients are mentored into a role. The Hotel School is now on its ninth course, with 10-15 people on each. It functions in a room in the basement of The Passage.

Two of the Hotel School graduates are featured in this book - Reyhaneh on page 213 and Adam on page 23.

So far as Zoe knows, at least 70% of them are still in full-time employment and if they can hold down a job for six months, they have probably cracked the difficulty of getting back into full-time work.

Serves 4

4 large pears
or 8 small ones

500ml elderberry
cordial, unsweetened

200g sugar

1 cinnamon stick

A couple of bay leaves

Zest and juice
of 1 lemon

PEARS IN ELDERBERRY SYRUP

Camilla Plum

This is a very Nordic take on the French and Italian pears in red wine. It has a beautiful autumnal feel to it and a surprising, rich flavour.

The elderberry cordial can be replaced with other fruit juices like cherry, blackberry, lingonberry, mulberry or blackcurrant; just adjust the sweetening.

———

Peel the pears, but leave the stalk on. Place them in a deep, heavy pot, and pour add the rest of the ingredients. Set the pan over a low heat and simmer till the pears are tender, turning them gently once in a while.

Remove the pears with a slotted spoon, then reduce the liquid to a thick syrup and taste for sweetness; the acidity of the pears varies, and this dessert needs to be sweet, but not too sweet. Allow the syrup to cool.

Arrange the pears in a deep, pretty dish, pour over the syrup and serve cold as they are.

The Passage

'It is a scandal that, in the 21st century, people are sleeping out on the streets of the UK. While people may find themselves at risk of homelessness, ending up on the street should not be inevitable and must be ended.'

MANGO & COCONUT YOGURT TRIFLE

Annie Bell

As a seven-year-old child I recall how, one assembly at school, Shelter came to give us an address, accompanied by a young single mother. She had just been provided with a flat to live in, after years of the uncertainty of being homeless and in hostels. Her face lit up as she described how she couldn't stop baking, far more fairy cakes and buns than she could ever give away, it was such a pleasure to have a kitchen to cook in. It has always stayed with me, how the fine dividing line between having a home, or not, is made up of an array of what amount to privileges, that we take for granted. So this recipe is dedicated to that young woman, and her children, and all others who have experienced the loss of a home that means so much.

This has the deep, sweet creamy layers we anticipate in a trifle, but one look at the ingredient list reveals how light and healthy it is. Lots of blueberries, mango and granola, while yogurt is that much more nutritious than cream. So you can dig deep without guilt.

———————

Place the gelatine strips in a large bowl, cover with cold water and soak for 5 minutes, then drain. Set the bowl over a pan with a little simmering water in it, pour over a few tablespoons of boiling water and stir to dissolve. Whizz the two yogurts, the mango flesh, lemon zest and juice and the stevia in a food processor until smooth. Transfer this to a large bowl. Stir about 4 tablespoons of the mango yogurt into the gelatine, one at a time, then stir this back in with the remainder. Cover and chill for 2–3 hours until lightly set or the consistency of whipped cream – start checking after 2 hours, and give it a little longer if it seems too loose.

To assemble the trifle, scatter half the blueberries over the base of a 20cm trifle bowl approx. 8cm deep, then scatter over half the granola. Smooth half the mango yogurt on top then repeat the layers. Cover and chill for several hours or overnight until set. Shortly before serving, decorate the top with strips of mango, coconut shavings and tiny mint leaves.

TIP
The best route to thin strips of mango is to cut a flat slice off the peeled fruit either side of and as close to the stone as possible, and then place the slices flat on the board and cut downwards into strips.

Serves 6–8

6 gelatine leaves, cut into broad strips

500g 0%-fat Greek yogurt

200g coconut yogurt

450g mango flesh (approx. 3 mangoes)

Finely grated zest of 1 lemon, plus 2 teaspoons juice

10g powdered stevia (if you want to keep the calories down; otherwise, use caster sugar to taste, if you prefer)

400g blueberries, plus a few to decorate

100g granola, eg Biona Pure Oaty

To decorate:
1 mango, peeled, cut into long thin strips (see tip)

Toasted coconut shavings

Tiny mint leaves

DOLCE FEDERICO

Fred Plotkin

Serves 2

4 slices panettone, cut into pieces 5cm wide and 2.5cm high

2 x 15g pieces unsalted butter

2 teaspoons bitter orange marmalade

1 bar (100g) good milk chocolate, possibly with hazelnuts or hazelnut filling, broken in small pieces

120ml full-fat or semi-skimmed milk

A recipe that is very simple and famously delicious. This makes two servings and you can make more just by multiplying the quantities. You can use fresh panettone but the result is even better if the panettone is a bit stale.

———

After cutting the panettone to size, toast the pieces slightly until they are warm and fragrant but not crunchy.

Place one piece of panettone on each of two dessert plates. Gently spread half the butter on each and let it melt, and top this with a teaspoon of bitter orange marmalade on the butter. Then place another piece of toasted panettone on top of each.

Combine the chocolate pieces and milk in a saucepan or double boiler. Heat gently and stir until the chocolate has melted and you have a warm sauce. Do not let it boil! Pour half of the sauce over each panettone and serve. Enjoy!

The Passage Vincentian values

'We are a voice for change and justice.'

CARAMEL THAI BANANAS

Daniel Green

I've been so very fortunate that my cooking has allowed me to travel to so many exciting destinations. By far Thailand is at the top of that list. I love the flavour of coconut milk and it matches so well with bananas. Bananas are a great source of potassium, which is perfect for a healthy diet. I've always been on a mission to create healthy food that is low in fat and this dessert is a good example.

For people that don't have the simple privileges that we take for granted, a meal is sometimes the best part of their day. The compassion of volunteers around the world who feed the homeless are doing so much more than just providing a meal. They are taking care and nurturing someone. It's a show of love when we cook for people.

We all need that.

―――――

Peel and slice the bananas about 3cm thick on an angle.

Heat a large non-stick frying pan over a medium heat. Add the brown sugar and water. Stir to dissolve. Add the bananas and cook for 3–4 minutes, then pour in the coconut milk and cook for 1 minute more. Stir in well; remove the heat and place in a serving dish.

Spoon the ricotta cheese on top and sprinkle with remaining tablespoon of brown sugar.

Serves 4

4 ripe bananas

100g brown sugar, plus an extra 1 tablespoon

60ml water

125ml light or low-fat coconut milk

250g low-fat ricotta cheese

HONEY ROAST FIGS WITH BLACK PEPPER MASCARPONE

Rich Harris

The heady aroma of fig trees instantly transports me to summer, when the plump, scarlet-centred fruits are at their very best. This pudding is lazy cooking at its finest; throw a parcel of figs onto the dying embers of the barbecue, serve with a spoonful of pepper-flecked mascarpone, and you'll be rewarded with something far better than the sum of its parts. If figs aren't your thing, swap in blackberries or cherries; both perfect partners to the warming spice of the black pepper.

———

If you're making this on the barbecue, let the coals die down a little so the heat isn't too fierce (or if you're cooking on gas just turn it down to medium).

Trim the stalks from the figs and cut each in half lengthways. Lay out a large sheet of foil, butter one half and lay the figs on top, cut side up. Drizzle the honey over the figs then fold the empty half of foil over the top and seal the edges to make a neat parcel. Lay on the grill and cook for 10 minutes. Alternatively lay the parcel in an ovenproof frying pan, set over a high heat for a couple of minutes then slide into a hot oven – around 200ºC/180ºC fan/Gas 6 – for 10 minutes.

While the figs are cooking, beat the mascarpone, icing sugar and pepper together until smooth.

Serve strewn with the pine nuts and a drizzle of extra virgin olive oil.

Serves 4

6 large ripe figs

Small knob of butter

2 tablespoons orange blossom honey or other floral honey

For the mascarpone:
150g mascarpone

1 tablespoon icing sugar

½ teaspoon freshly ground black pepper

To serve:
2 tablespoons pine nuts, toasted

Extra virgin olive oil

BAKED CHEESECAKE

Nadiya Hussain

Serves 9

For the cheesecake:
Butter, for greasing

900g full-fat cream cheese

200g caster sugar

150ml soured cream

3 tablespoons plain flour

3 medium eggs, beaten

2 teaspoons vanilla bean paste

For the honey-salted caramel:
50g butter

170g set honey

300ml double cream

½ teaspoon salt

For the tiffin crumble:
150g digestive biscuits, roughly crushed (try putting them in a zip-lock bag and bashing them with a rolling pin)

75g unsalted butter, melted

30g Demerara sugar

50g dark chocolate chips or chunks

50g toasted hazelnuts, roughly chopped

There's a homeless lady I used to see every time I went shopping. I would give her something from my trolley and some spare change and walk off. Other times I was too busy even to bend down and hand over food or change. One day, I parked up my trolley, opened a bag of crisps and sat with her. We spoke about the weather, how she got there, and about our dreams. We laughed and then I went home. Let's not walk past. Let's stop, talk and provide the gift of time, because homeless people are not invisible and neither are their problems.

A simple baked cheesecake is one of my favourite desserts. It can sit in the fridge and be enjoyed over the course of a week, and that ultimate slice is the best slice of all. But sometimes I feel short-changed by the base. So here I've baked a cheesecake without any base at all, and instead topped it with honey salted caramel and a chocolaty tiffin mixture. It's essentially a flipped-over version of the classic, but in my opinion all the best cakes are a little back to front!

———————

Preheat the oven to 160°C/140°C fan/Gas 3. Grease the base of a 20cm round tin (not loose-bottomed, imagine the leakage!) and line it with baking paper.

Put all the cheesecake ingredients in a large bowl and mix, just for 1 minute or so, until well combined. You don't want to mix for too long and incorporate any air.

Pour the mixture into the lined tin, tap it on the worktop to release any trapped air, then level the surface. Bake on the lower shelf of the oven for 1 hour. Once the hour is up, open the oven door and wedge a wooden spoon in the door to keep it just open and let out the heat slowly. Turn the oven off but don't remove the cheesecake until the oven is completely cold – only then put the cheesecake into the fridge to chill overnight.

The next day, make the honey-salted caramel. Melt the butter in a small pan over a medium heat. Add the honey and cook over a medium-high heat for 10 minutes, until the caramel is a golden brown. If it starts to catch, turn the heat down slightly. After 10 minutes, pour in the cream, give it a mix and allow it to just come up to the boil. Take off the heat and stir in the salt. Set aside.

To make the tiffin crumble, empty the roughly crushed biscuits into a bowl and pour over the melted butter. Leave to cool for 10 minutes, then add the sugar, chocolate and hazelnuts. Turn out the cheesecake onto a serving plate or platter. Loosely pile the tiffin mixture on top of the cheesecake.

Reheat the caramel if it has cooled too much, and pour over the cheesecake. For any of you who have had past cheesecakes fly across the table from the sheer brute force of fighting to cut a tight biscuit base, you are welcome!

Recipe taken from Nadiya's Family Favourites *(Michael Joseph, £22)*

Serves 4

For the base:
40g hazelnuts

150g digestive
biscuits

50g unsalted butter

40g honey

For the cheesecake:
2 leaves gelatine

250g double cream

250g mascarpone

150ml elderflower
cordial

Zest and juice
of 1 lemon

For the gooseberries:
200ml water

125g caster sugar

200g fresh
gooseberries

ELDERFLOWER & GOOSEBERRY CHEESECAKE

Emily Watkins

Cheesecake is a huge favourite in our family but I love adapting it to suit the seasons. The addition of elderflower and gooseberries is deliciously fragrant and floral and perfect on a warm late spring day. Once the small gooseberry window closes, you can garnish the cheesecake with fresh raspberries or strawberries. I use a 22cm fluted, loose-bottomed tart tin for this.

———

Preheat the oven to 180ºC/160ºC fan/Gas 4.

First make the base: put the hazelnuts on a baking tray and toast in the oven for 8 minutes. Crush the digestives in a bag with a rolling pin, then tip them into a bowl with the hazelnuts, also broken up.

In a small saucepan, bring the butter and honey to the boil and pour into the nuts and biscuits. Mix well. Line a 22cm cake tin with parchment paper and press the mix into the base. Place in the fridge to harden.

Meanwhile, make the filling: soak the gelatine in cold water. Pour a couple of tablespoons of the cream into a small saucepan. Bring to a simmer and add the softened gelatine. Stir to dissolve. Slowly add the rest of the cream, then pour it all into a bowl. Add the mascarpone, elderflower cordial, lemon zest and juice to the cream and then whisk until it forms stiff ribbons.

Pour the mix over the base and tap on the bottom so it settles into all the gaps. Place back in the fridge to set for at least 6 hours.

For the gooseberries, put the water and sugar in a saucepan and bring to the boil. Simmer for 2 minutes, drop the gooseberries into the simmering syrup and turn off the heat but leave the pan on the hot hob, allowing the gooseberries to come to room temperature.

Serve the elderflower cheesecake with the poached gooseberries.

ORIGINAL BAKED LEMON & SULTANA CHEESECAKE

Anne-Marie Batson

My love affair with cheesecakes began in childhood. My mum made cheesecake for dessert for Sunday family lunch. My absolute favourite? A soft, thick layer of cream cheese, with a crushed digestive biscuit base, unbaked, topped with sliced strawberries and drizzled with coulis. Delicious.

Cheesecake has a rich history. A form of cheesecake may have been popular in ancient Greece back in 2000 BC, used for religious purposes. After passing through Roman times, a modern cheesecake version was found in an old English cookbook from Henry VIII's time. The recipe hit American shores in the 1800s, adding cream cheese to the recipe.

Cheesecake is either baked or unbaked. And, did you know there is a variety of recipes depending on which continent? Asian-style cheesecakes are light and spongy, flavoured with mango and lychee. North Americans love unbaked cheesecakes, even twice-baked ones, while Europe has too many fantastic varieties to mention.

Here's an extremely tasty cheesecake. Back in the day, I loved making desserts especially cheesecakes when I had the time. Perhaps in a previous life, I worked as a pastry chef. Nowadays, cheesecake is wonderful yet occasional treat for me. Enjoy!

———

Preheat oven to 190ºC/170ºC fan/Gas 5. Place the biscuits in a strong plastic bag and crush with a rolling pin. Mix with the melted butter and press into the base of a 20cm springform cake tin. Pop into the freezer for 5 minutes or so to set.

Using electric beaters, mix together the mascarpone, crème fraîche, egg yolks, caster sugar and cornflour until well blended. Stir in the sultanas and lemon zest and spoon over the crumb base, smoothing over the surface.

Place on a baking sheet and bake for 40 minutes until golden. It will be fairly wobbly but don't worry, it will set as it cools. The cake sometimes cracks, but you can avoid this by allowing it to cool slowly – turn off the oven, open the door and leave it to cool as the oven does.

When completely cool, place in the fridge for at least 1–2 hours but preferably overnight. Carefully remove from the tin and dust with icing sugar. Slice into wedges and serve with a drizzle of cream.

Serves 6

For the base:
150g digestive biscuits

50g butter, melted

For the cheesecake:
500g mascarpone

200g crème fraîche

2 egg yolks

100g caster sugar

2 tablespoons cornflour

75g golden sultanas

Grated zest of 1 lemon

Icing sugar for dusting

Cream to serve

SHIR BERENJ

Reyhaneh Niroomand

Serves 6-8

175g broken pudding rice (preferably scented Iranian rice)

1 teaspoon salt

1.9 litres whole milk

150-200g granulated sugar

1 tablespoon slivered almonds

1 teaspoon ground cardamom

225ml rose water

120ml fresh double cream

Pistachios and dried rose buds to decorate

Shir berenj is served as breakfast, during afternoon tea or as a dessert. Sugar is not always added; instead it can be served with jam, syrup, honey or date syrup. This dish is cooked all over Iran and, if served with no sugar and a bit of honey, is given to the elderly or young kids because it doesn't need to be chewed and it is nourishing as it has rice and milk.

———

Wash the crushed rice and soak it in cold water to cover, with the salt, overnight. Strain next day and rinse twice under running water.

Put the milk in a large pan, add the rice and bring to the boil; cover and turn down the heat and gently cook the rice until tender and the milk has evaporated.

Then add the sugar, almonds and ground cardamom and cook for 30 minutes, stirring to prevent the rice sticking to the pan. Pour in the rose water and cream, stirring until the mixture is thick and not runny, about as runny as normal rice pudding. Turn off the heat and put the lid on the saucepan, covering it with a teacloth to absorb any moisture; leave for 10 minutes. Pour into individual serving bowls and decorate with the pistachios and rose buds. Chill in the fridge to set for 45 minutes to 1 hour.

Reyhaneh Niroomand - Hotel School

Reyhaneh got a job as a chef in a group when she arrived from Iran in 2005; it was badly managed and folded after a couple of years. She'd worked as a traditional artist in Mashhad; her husband is a heating engineer. Life in England was very different for them. She has always cooked for her family and her ambition had been to set up a company.

She came to the Hotel School in Victoria in 2018 for a three-month course. It gave her the confidence to set up her own baking business with her 26-year-old daughter, *Fat Cat Bakes Ltd*. Initially they worked from home but are now looking for premises as the business takes off. They are based in Finchley. She loves it and is always working out how to help women, her friends. She cooks Persian cuisine and volunteers in the kitchen at Sufra, a charity in Brent serving the homeless.

Reyhaneh is vegan, and a diabetic. She makes her own bread, adding honey or date syrup, cumin and herbs with coconut flour. She is considering raw veganism but it is very difficult. But business is booming and The Passage uses her too when they need cakes for special occasions. She is a go-getter. She will succeed.

Serves 6–8

175g crushed rice

1 teaspoon salt

1.4 litres water

300g granulated sugar

50g butter

1 teaspoon ground cardamom

2 tablespoons slivered almonds

1 teaspoon saffron strands, crushed and soaked in 4 tablespoons hot water for 10 minutes

75ml rose water

Ground cinnamon, pistachio nuts or dried rose buds to decorate

SHOLE ZARD

Reyhaneh Niroomand

Shole zard is served usually during religious ceremonies, such as the anniversary of a close relative's death or on Islamic holy days. It is usually prepared in massive pots and given out to neighbours and guests or taken to the mosque (large pots serve around 100 or more portions). It is served as afternoon tea or dessert.

Just like *Shir berenj* (see page 213) it is served across Iran and the main difference between them is that *Shole zard* doesn't have milk or cream but it does get its golden colour from saffron. *Shole zard* is usually served only if there is a religious holiday or an occasion but *Shir berenj* is served whenever someone fancies it.

———

Follow the instructions for cooking the rice in *Shir berenj*. Then cook the rice with the water in a large saucepan, bringing it to the boil and turning it down to simmering point. When the rice is half cooked, stir in the sugar and continue cooking, mixing quite often for an hour to prevent the rice sticking to the pan.

Add the butter, cardamoms, almonds and saffron and cook for a further 30 minutes until the mixture is thick. Pour in the rose water and cook for a final 15 minutes and remove from the heat.

Follow the instructions of *Shir berenj* to finish the dish and serve it.

AUNT ANNA'S LECHE FRITA

Carlos Horrillo

The recipe takes me back to a safe warm place; a place that sadly can seem so far away for some people. I always wonder what lies behind some people's homelessness and how we, as a society, can let so many slip through undetected yet let them exist in plain sight.

———————

You need a 25–30cm heavy-based frying pan and a rectangular enamel cake tin/tray about 30 x 22.5cm (much bigger and the mixture will spread too thinly. Lightly coat the rectangular tin with olive oil.

Pour 250ml of the milk into a bowl and add the flour and cornflour (you can dissolve the cornflour first in a little cold water). Beat with a hand whisk or a hand-held mixer until smooth. You can also sieve the mixture before setting it aside.

Pour the rest of the milk into a saucepan, along with the cinnamon sticks and nutmeg. Bring to the boil and then reduce the heat to low and add the sugar, stirring until it is dissolved. Remove the cinnamon sticks. Add the flour mixture to the milk pan. Increase the heat to medium and cook for 20 minutes, stirring constantly until smooth and creamy. Transfer the mixture to the prepared tin. Allow it to cool to room temperature, then cover and refrigerate.

Once set, cut into approximately 5cm squares.

Prepare two shallow plates, one with plain flour, the other with the eggs. Whisk the eggs until blended.

Pour 125ml of olive oil into your frying pan. Place over a medium heat. While the oil is heating, coat the squares, carefully and completely, in flour, shaking off any excess, then dip into eggs.

Do the next stage in batches. Add a few squares to the hot oil. Reduce the heat to low and fry for 1 minute on each side or until golden. Once done, transfer to a large plate with some kitchen paper to soak up the excess oil. Repeat with the remaining squares, always bringing the oil back up to temperature before frying.

Before serving, dust with sugar, cinnamon and nutmeg (optional). These can be served warm or at room temperature.

**Serves 4
(makes 20 squares
or thereabouts)**

750ml full-fat milk
or full-fat oat milk

45g plain flour, plus
some for dusting

50g cornflour

1½ cinnamon sticks

2 generous pinches
ground nutmeg, plus
extra to serve
(optional)

2 eggs

125ml olive oil

To serve:
125g white sugar or,
if you have a sweet
tooth, then pile on
another 10g!
Or, for a healthier
option, you can reduce
the sugar

Ground cinnamon
for sprinkling

The people listed below, from actors to chefs to Passage staff, volunteers and clients, have all contributed recipes to this book. The Passage community would like to thank them for taking part in this project, and for sharing their recipes with us.

————

Darina Allen

co-founded Ballymaloe Cookery School in Co. Cork, which has won several international awards. She is the author of many cookbooks, including *Ballymaloe Cookery Course* and *One Pot Feeds All*.

Nancy Almeida

is a client of The Passage, supported by its 'Home for Good' befriending scheme. She grew up in Sweden and started cooking to help her maintain a more positive lifestyle.

Kimiko Barber

teaches Japanese cooking and contributes to *The Financial Times*. Her broadcasting work includes Radio 4's *The Food Programme* and BBC One's *Saturday Kitchen*. She has written many cookbooks, from *The Chopstick Diet* to *YO! Sushi: The Japanese Cookbook*.

Karen Barnes

has been Editor of *delicious* magazine (deliciousmagazine.co.uk) since 2010. She is obsessive about food, cooking and writing recipes. Her mission is to get more people into the kitchen to discover the rewards of cooking.

Anne-Marie Batson

is a broadcaster, host and presenter. Her clients include BBC Radio 5 Live Sports Extra and talkSPORT. She is passionate about sport, championing for equality in the sports space as well as gender rights and social issues.

Annie Bell

is a nutritionist, author and journalist who has been cookery writer for *The Mail on Sunday*'s *YOU Magazine* for over 20 years. She has written numerous cookbooks, including *Plant Power* and *Low Carb Revolution*.

Mary Berry

has been teaching the nation to cook for over four decades. She is one of our favourite bakers and the author of over 70 books. She was a judge on *The Great British Bake Off* and is now one of the judges of *Britain's Best Home Cook*. In 2012 Mary was awarded a CBE and continues to inspire people to enjoy home cooking.

Richard Bertinet

is a Breton baker who now bakes and teaches in Bath. He won BBC Food Champion of the Year in 2010 and has revolutionised home baking with his books *Dough* and *Crust*.

Monisha Bharadwaj

is a chef and award-winning author who has contributed to many shows from BBC Two's *Food and Drink* to Radio 4's *Food Programme*. She started her school, Cooking with Monisha, in London, in 2004, which teaches her brand of simple authentic Indian cooking.

Cherie Blair

is founder of the Cherie Blair Foundation for Women. She is an international human rights lawyer, a campaigner for women's equality and wife of former British Prime Minister Tony Blair.

Micky Bottone

is Chef of the hostel Passage House.

Gyles Brandreth

is a writer, broadcaster, actor, former MP and now Chancellor of the University of Chester. He has appeared on many programmes from *Countdown* and *Just a Minute* to *Celebrity Gogglebox* and *QI*.

Rory Bremner

is known for his satirical programmes and impressions of Prime Ministers and Presidents from John Major to Donald Trump. He first became involved with The Passage in 1998, doing fundraising events and helping launch the hostel Passage House. He regularly hosted the *Night Under The Stars* concert from its beginning in 2001.

Giancarlo & Katie Caldesi

Giancarlo, a successful restaurateur and cookery-school owner, was forced to transform his life when he was diagnosed with Type 2 diabetes and a severe gluten intolerance. He and his wife Katie developed gluten-free alternatives to pasta and bread and co-authored *The Diabetes Weight-loss Cookbook*.

Samantha Cameron

was Creative Director of Smythson until 2010. After six years in Downing Street as the wife of former British Prime Minister David Cameron, she founded the fashion label Cefinn in 2017. An ambassador for *Save the Children,* she took part in the *Great Sport Relief Bake Off* in 2016.

Massimo Cartino

is a client of The Passage who has now been helped to move into his own accommodation.

Mick Clarke

started his career as a youth worker and has been CEO of The Passage since 2009. He ensures the organisation grows and develops to meet the ever-changing needs of the clients.

Gino D'Acampo

is an Italian chef best known for his food-focused TV shows and cookbooks, including *Gino's Italian Escape*. He is also a rapidly expanding restaurateur.

Nour Dakoba

has been Chef at The Passage for the last 19 years.

Claudette Dawkins

has been Head Chef at The Passage for 21 years.

Hussien Dekmak

was born in Beirut and has been cooking since he was a teenager. He opened his Camden restaurant Le Mignon in 1997 and subsequently published *The Lebanese Cookbook*. He is now chef at Mezza Me in Brixton.

David Dimbleby

is a journalist and presenter of current affairs and political programmes. He is best known for the BBC's long-running *Question Time*. He has also hosted coverage of the UK's general elections since 1979.

Liz Earle

is a multi-brand founder who has worked in the world of wellbeing since the 1980s. The best-selling author of over 30 books on living and eating well, she's Editor-in-Chief of *Liz Earle Wellbeing* magazine and hosts the popular *Liz Earle Wellbeing Show* podcast. In 2007, Liz was awarded an MBE.

Caroline Eden

is a writer and critic contributing to *The Guardian*, *Financial Times* and *Times Literary Supplement*. Her latest book, *Black Sea*, fuses travel with recipes and has won awards including the Art of Eating Prize.

Maria Elia

became head chef at Delfina and The Whitechapel Gallery Dining Room. She wrote *The Modern Vegetarian*, *Full of Flavour* and *Smashing Plates* and has appeared on TV and in magazines.

Julie Etchingham

is a journalist and, since 2008, newsreader with ITV's *News at Ten*. She has presented the current affairs programme *Tonight* since 2010. She is also patron of the London homeless charity Caritas Anchor House.

Josephine Fairley

co-founded Green & Black's in 1991 and built the brand into the world's leading organic chocolate. An award-winning author and journalist, she co-wrote *The Beauty Bible* and *Sweet Dreams*. For the past 20 years she has been involved with Centrepoint, the London homeless charity.

Julian Fellowes

is an actor and writer best known for the Academy Award-winning *Gosford Park* and the smash-hit TV series *Downton Abbey*. Along with many other film, stage and TV projects he has written several books.

Giana Ferguson

is a cheesemaker based on a family farm in West Cork. She is the author of *Gubbeen: The Story of a Working Farm and its Foods*.

Mark Flanagan

is Head Chef at Buckingham Palace. He has written *A Royal Cookbook* and *Royal Teas*.

Bob Flowerdew

is an organic gardener and television and radio presenter. He is a regular panel member of Radio 4's *Gardeners' Question Time* as well as contributing to many magazines.

Sadie Frost

is an actress, producer and fashion designer. She ran her fashion label FrostFrench until 2011. She has written for publications including *Harper's* and co-authored *Nourish*. Sadie is patron for the Hepatitis C Trust.

Stephen Fry

is an actor, comedian and writer. Best known for his TV comedy including *Blackadder*, *A Bit of Fry & Laurie* and *QI*, he has also written four novels, three volumes of autobiography and is the voice behind all seven *Harry Potter* audiobooks.

Georgina Fuggle

is a chef, food stylist, editor and author. She writes a blog, *Fuggle Antics*, and runs a sustainable jewellery brand, Little by Little, which uses ingredients as design inspiration.

Yohanis Gebreyesus

is an Ethiopian chef who founded the restaurant Antica in Addis Ababa. His Chef Yohanis brand promotes a healthy lifestyle using Ethiopian produce. Over 26 million people watch his weekly food programmes on YouTube. Yohanis co-wrote *Ethiopia* with Jeff Koehler, which won a James Beard Award in 2020.

Oliver Gladwin

is one of a trio of brothers who have brought their Local & Wild concept to the city with their restaurants The Shed, Rabbit, Nutbourne and Sussex. Oliver is the chef and creative inspiration across the business. He started his wild food journey at the River Cottage.

Jeremy Goring

is CEO of London's Goring Hotel. He co-founded the Hotel School with Mick Clarke. The school teaches hospitality skills to homeless and vulnerable people, matches them to employment, and supports them in their first steps into work.

Daniel Green

is an international TV personality and author also known as The Model Cook. He is a healthy eating expert, whose books include *The Paleo Diet* and *Healthy Eating for Lower Cholesterol*.

Henrietta Green

is a food writer, journalist, consultant, event organiser and champion of British speciality foods. She published *Food Lovers' Guide to Britain*, campaigned for farmers markets and founded the British Charcuterie Live Awards in 2018.

Will Greenwood

is a former rugby union player and member of the 2003 World Cup winning squad. He is now an analyst for Sky Sports and *The Telegraph*. He is a patron for Child Bereavement UK and Borne.

John Gregory-Smith

is an author, presenter, food and travel writer who specialises in Middle Eastern and North African cuisine. His books include *Saffron in the Souks* and *Orange Blossom & Honey*. He has a regular column in *The Daily Telegraph*.

Rich Harris

is a passionate chef who has worked behind the scenes on the UK's leading food programmes. He has written two books, *Fire & Smoke* and *Root & Leaf*.

Diana Henry

is *The Sunday Telegraph*'s food writer and has a column in *Stella* magazine. She has won many awards as a food writer and is the author of twelve books.

Shaun Hill

is one of Britain's enduringly successful chef and an accomplished food writer. The Merchant House was his Michelin-starred restaurant that put Ludlow on the gastronomic map. He currently holds a Michelin star at The Walnut Tree in Wales.

Tom Holland

is an award-winning historian, biographer and broadcaster. His most recent book is *Dominion: The Making of the Western Mind*. He is a presenter on Radio 4's *Making History* and has written and presented a number of TV documentaries on subjects ranging from ISIS to dinosaurs.

Ken Hom

is a chef and TV presenter for the classic BBC series *Ken Hom's Chinese Cookery*. The accompanying book was a bestseller. Since 2008 he has been an ambassador for Action Against Hunger.

Carlos Horrillo,

with Patrick Morcas, owned El Parador in Camden, a family-run restaurant that served simple tapas for over 20 years. Customers returned time and again and their book *Tapas* showcases many simple and classic recipes.

Ching-he Huang,

known as 'Ching', is an Emmy-nominated, award-winning TV chef and cookbook author, who has been championing, popularising and de-mystifying Chinese cuisine in the media, since 2003. She is the author of nine books. Her new book, *Asian Green*, is out in January 2021. More info @chinghehuang

Nadiya Hussain

rose to fame after winning *The Great British Bake Off in 2015*. She has since written five cookbooks as well as story/cookbooks for children. She writes a monthly column for *The Times* and has hosted many BBC TV shows.

Ghillie James

was food editor for *Sainsbury's Magazine* and now writes from her home in Singapore for various magazines, including *delicious*. She is the author of *Amazing Grains* and *Jam, Jelly and Relish*. Ghillie's latest book, *The Little Grower's Cookbook*, is coming out in spring 2021.

Daniel Katwala

is a trained chef and sommelier in training. He works at The Gate in Richmond, Surrey.

Sue Lawley

is one of Britain's best-known broadcasters. Her career covers television news, current affairs and chat shows. She presented Radio 4's *Desert Island Discs* from 1988 to 2006 and chaired the BBC's *Reith Lectures* for 18 years.

Nigella Lawson

has been teaching us about the pleasures of the table since her first book, *How to Eat*, in 1998. Several bestselling titles later, and accompanying TV series, have made her a household name around the world.

Jeremy Lee

is chef proprietor at London restaurant Quo Vadis, having previously been at the Blueprint Café. He has also had a successful food-writing career.

Elisabeth Luard

is a food writer whose books include *European Peasant Cookery* and *The Food of Spain and Portugal*. She is a regular contributor to newspapers and magazines and Chair of The Oxford Symposium on Food and Cookery. Her *Preserving, Potting and Pickling* is just published.

Andrew Marr

is a journalist, television and radio presenter. Formerly editor of *The Independent* and political editor for *BBC News*, he is now best known for *The Andrew Marr* Show on Sunday mornings. He is the author of several books, including *A History of Modern Britain*.

Spencer Matthews

is an original cast member of the award-winning TV series *Made in Chelsea*. He is the founder and CEO of The Clean Liquor Co.

Paul McCartney

is a legendary musician and songwriter who gained worldwide fame in The Beatles. His unrivalled career has made him a well-respected entertainer and an internationally regarded public figure.

Robert McCullough

is a Vice President of Penguin Random House Canada. Through his imprint, Appetite, he publishes books that celebrate food, drink and lifestyle.

Allegra McEvedy

is a chef, writer and broadcaster who lives by the philosophy that good food should be available to everyone. She co-founded LEON, has been a judge on *Junior Bake Off*, and has written numerous books, including *Quick, Quick Slow*.

Jekka McVicar

is an organic grower of herbs and horticultural author, designer and consultant. She is renowned for her passion and knowledge of herbs. Jekka is a judge and ambassador for the RHS and author of seven books including *Jekka's Complete Herb Book*.

Thomasina Miers

co-founded the Mexican-inspired street food chain Wahaca. She won the first series of *Masterchef* in 2005. She writes for the *Saturday Guardian* magazine, has presented several TV programmes and written seven cookbooks, the latest being *Home Cook*.

Julia Neuberger

is a crossbench peer, social commentator and writer. She is involved in many voluntary roles and her latest book is *Antisemitism: What It Is. What It Isn't. Why It Matters.*

Chantelle Nicholson

is the award-winning Chef Owner of Tredwells and the author of *Planted: A Chef's Show-Stopping Vegan Recipes.*

Reyhaneh Niroomand

arrived from Iran in 2005. After a course at the Hotel School she set up her own baking business with her daughter, Fat Cat Bakes Ltd.

Jill Norman

is an award-winning editor, publisher and author of books on food. She writes frequently on food and wine, and is a regular speaker on gastronomy at literary and food festivals.

Rory O'Connell

co-founded the Ballymaloe Cookery School in 1983 with his sister, Darina Allen. He was head chef at Ballymaloe House for ten years and twice awarded Ireland's Chef of the Year. He is the author of *Master It* and *Cook Well, Eat Well.*

Alison Oakervee

Alison Oakervee is Food Editor for Waitrose & Partners. She also edited *Share: The Women for Women Cookbook.*

Antonio Orlando

has been a trustee of The Passage since 2015. He was Chairman of *Night Under The Stars* between 2011 and 2018 and works in classical music.

Martha Ortiz

is a renowned chef who is inspired by her native Mexico. She has two restaurants, Dulce Patria in Mexico City and Ella Canta in London.

Yotam Ottolenghi

is a chef and food writer. He is the owner of six delis and restaurants in London, writes for *The Guardian*, and is the author of several bestselling cookbooks, including *Ottolenghi* and *Simple.*

Nathan Outlaw

is the king of fish with a restaurant in Port Isaac. It holds two Michelin stars and was crowned Britain's number 1 restaurant by *The Good Food Guide* in 2018 and 2019. His many cookbooks allow you to recreate some of his famous recipes.

Camellia Panjabi

is the author of the world's bestselling curry book *50 Great Curries of India.* She is Group Director at Masala World which has seven Masala Zone restaurants in central London, and three fine-dining establishments, Chutney Mary, Amaya and Veeraswamy.

Tom Parker Bowles

is a respected food writer and critic. He writes for *The Mail on Sunday* and *Esquire* and is regularly seen on television as a judge. His books include *Full English*, which won a Guild of Food Writers Award in 2010.

Roger Phillips

is a celebrated mushroom forager and award-winning photographer of the world's garden plants. He has written over 30 books, including *The Worldwide Forager.*

Charlotte Pike

is the author of five cookery books, a leading independent cookery teacher and chef, running Charlotte's Kitchen, a private catering company. She has a passion for good, seasonal, uncomplicated home cooking.

José Pizarro

is regarded as one of the best Spanish chefs in the UK, with four restaurants. A favourite on many TV programmes, including the BBC's *Saturday Kitchen*, he has written *Seasonal Spanish Food, Andalusia* and many more.

Fred Plotkin

is one of America's foremost experts on opera and everything Italian. He has worked at La Scala and the Metropolitan Opera, written books, including *Italy for the Gourmet Traveller*, and appears regularly on the BBC.

Camilla Plum

is a Danish chef who has been championing organic healthy food since her first cookbook in 1983. She has her own TV programme in Denmark, and runs an organic farm near Copenhagen that is open to visitors.

Glynn Purnell,

affectionately known as the Yummie Brummie, is the owner and head chef at Purnell's Restaurant in Birmingham, which was awarded a Michelin star in 2009. He has taken part in the BBC's *Great British Menu* and is regularly seen on *Saturday Kitchen.*

Theo Randall

is a chef inspired by Italian cuisine. He spent ten years at River Café, earning a Michelin star along the way. In 2006 he launched his own restaurant in London at the InterContinental. He is the author of *Pasta* and *My Simple Italian.*

Franco Randone & Marta Khabalaeva

Franco Randone is a money adviser at The Passage. His wife Marta Khabalaeva is a Georgian/Russian doctor. They now have their own YouTube channel which attracts over 30,000 followers.

Annie Rigg

is an experienced writer and stylist. A Leith's-trained chef, she has since written 15 cookbooks, including *Pies and Tarts.* She regularly contributes to leading food and lifestyle magazines.

Claudia Roden

is a cookbook writer who has published multiple bestsellers, including the award-winning *The Book of Jewish Food.* She is also President of The Oxford Symposium on Food and Cookery.

Amber Rose

grew up in New Zealand surrounded by organic gardens and heritage produce. She has travelled the world cooking and lived in London as a food writer, private chef, and doula. Her books include *Love Bake Nourish* and *Wild Delicious.*

**Rude Health
(Rachel Higgins, Lewis
Macleod & Fergus Snell)**

Rude Health is an innovative food and drinks company based in London. Its philosophy is to make good food without adding anything fake or artificial. Its Ultimate Muesli was created in 2005 and has since been joined by a range of award-winning cereals, snacks and dairy-free drinks. Lewis Macleod and Rachel Higgins are chefs at The Rude Health Café in Fulham, London and Fergus Snell is Head Chef and Chief Barista.

Nick Sandler

is the Creative Chef for Farmer J, writes cookbooks and is a freelance recipe consultant.

Jon Snow

is a journalist best known as the longest-running presenter of *Channel 4 News*, which he has presented since 1989.

Sarah Stacey

has extensive experience in the health and beauty industries. She is co-editor, with Jo Fairley, of the bestselling *Beauty Bible* series. She was Health Editor of *The Mail on Sunday*'s *YOU Magazine* for 17 years.

Rick Stein

is a chef, restaurateur, author and TV presenter. He has written over 20 cookbooks and made over 30 TV programmes. The Seafood Restaurant in Padstow celebrated 40 years in 2015. In 2018 Rick was presented with a CBE.

Jeanne Strang

is the author of *Goose Fat & Garlic*. She and her husband have lived in southwest France for nearly 50 years, spending their time researching home cooking in the region.

Rebecca Sullivan

is a self-taught cook, food curator, sustainable living advocate, author, urban farmer and entrepreneur. She worked on the launch of the Real Food Festival in London and is passionate about heritage.

Rachel de Thample

is a cook, forager, preserver and urban gardener. She has worked at *Waitrose Food Illustrated* and as Head of Food at the organic box scheme Abel & Cole. She is the author of *Less Meat, More Veg*, *FIVE* and *Tonics & Teas*. Her latest is *Gifts from the Modern Larder*.

Susie Theodorou

is a food stylist and writer who has created recipes for *Bon Appétit*, *Martha Stewart Living* and *Waitrose Kitchen*. Her most recent book is *Mediterranean: Naturally Nourishing Recipes from the World's Healthiest Diet*.

Petroc Trelawny

is a classical music TV and radio presenter. Since 1998 he has presented Radio 3's *Breakfast* programme. He also presents the BBC Proms from the Royal Albert Hall. He has regularly hosted the annual *Night Under The Stars* Gala Concert in aid of The Passage.

Linda Tubby

is a food writer and stylist. Inspired by her travels as a fashion designer Linda now develops recipes for magazines and brings food to life for photography for many books as well as six of her own, which include *Cracked* and *Solo*.

Gregg Wallace

is a TV presenter, writer and former greengrocer. He is best known for co-presenting the BBC *Masterchef* series, as well *Eat Well for Less*. His autobiography, *Life on a Plate*, was published in 2012.

Emily Watkins

was chef and owner of The Kingham Plough in Gloucestershire until 2019. Previously she worked in Florence and at The Fat Duck under Heston Blumenthal. She was one of the winners of the *Great British Menu* in 2014.

John Whaite

won *The Great British Bake Off* in 2012 which enabled him to make baking a full-time job. He is now a successful food writer and cookery school teacher but is now training to be a lawyer. He has published five cookery books, of which *A Flash in the Pan* is the latest.

Vogue Williams

is a TV presenter, model and DJ known for participating in *Dancing with the Stars* and winning *Bear Grylls: Mission Survive*.

Antony Worrall Thompson

is a prolific cookery book writer with many of his titles focusing on food issues such as diabetes, health and nutrition. He owns and runs The Greyhound in Henley-on-Thames with his wife Jacinta, and has appeared on many TV programmes including the BBC's *Saturday Kitchen*.

paul a. young

is a chocolatier who has won numerous awards and has a reputation as an incredibly creative flavour alchemist. His book *Adventures with Chocolate* won the Best Chocolate Book award in the World Gourmands.

Acknowledgements

———

The compiler would like to thank all the contributors who so generously gave their recipes; such lovely and original ones. And those who have shared their stories and talked, giving their time unsparingly.

The book team included Ruth Tyson, who jumped at the job immediately and has been both creative and a joy to work with throughout the process; Nassima Rothacker who took the gorgeous food photography; Becks Wilkinson cooked and cooked beautifully for the food shots; Wei Tang, most amazing props stylist, who deftly moved with lightning speed in difficult circumstances and persuaded her husband, Adrian Phillips, to drive to Warwickshire twice. Maria Aversa so ably assisted Nassima and Lauren Miller chopped nobly for Becks on the last two days of the shoot in London. Thanks so much to all.

Many thanks too to the prop houses for their help and support for The Passage – amongst all are Karl at Tortoise Backgrounds, Jo Harris of Topham Street, Lucy Attwater at Prop Supply, Liz and Nick at China & Co, and Victoria Allen and David Munns.

Stephanie Evans did a most brilliant job in proofreading and ironing out errors, always so swiftly and with good humour, and contributed so much to the project. Altaimage London have generously helped with the repro of colour.

At The Passage, Mick Clarke and Emma Noble were always helpful and supportive, and acknowledgement should also be made to Thenuka Mahendra, Fran Hodge, Andrew Hollingsworth, Claudette Dawkins, Rachel Verralls and all those who had their photos taken.

On the publicity front, Jacqui Graham, Rosemary Trapnell and Suzi and Becca Smith of Sistersmith PR have been awesome. And to Julia Barder for a huge contribution on the sales side, thank you.

I am truly humbled by your contributions.

———

Mick Clarke, Chief Executive of The Passage, would like to thank Kyle Cathie for her immense support in bringing this book to life. Kyle created the original concept and has overseen every detail, working entirely in a voluntary capacity. Without her, it simply would not exist. And it is with sincere thanks to Kyle that every purchase of this special book will help The Passage in its mission to end street homelessness.